I0413107

Arsenic-Related Water Quality with Depth and Water Quality of Well-Head Samples from Production Wells, Oklahoma, 2008

By Carol J. Becker, S. Jerrod Smith, James R. Greer, and Kevin A. Smith

Prepared in cooperation with the Oklahoma Department of Environmental Quality and the Ground-Water Protection Council

Scientific Investigations Report 2010–5047

U.S. Department of the Interior
U.S. Geological Survey

U.S. Department of the Interior
KEN SALAZAR, Secretary

U.S. Geological Survey
Marcia K. McNutt, Director

U.S. Geological Survey, Reston, Virginia: 2010

This and other USGS information products are available at http://store.usgs.gov/
U.S. Geological Survey
Box 25286, Denver Federal Center
Denver, CO 80225

To learn about the USGS and its information products visit http://www.usgs.gov/
1-888-ASK-USGS

Suggested citation:
Becker, C.J., Smith, S.J., Greer, J.R., and Smith, K.A., 2010, Arsenic-related water quality with depth and water quality of well-head samples from production wells, Oklahoma, 2008: U.S. Geological Scientific Investigations Report 2010–5047, 38 p.

Contents

Figures

Tables

Conversion Factors, Datums, and Water-Quality Units

Inch/Pound to SI

Multiply	By	To obtain
Length		
inch (in)	0.39	centimeter (cm)
inch (in)	0.039	millimeter (mm)
foot (ft)	0.3048	meter (m)
mile (mi)	0.621	kilometer (km)
Volume		
gallon (gal)	0.264	liter (L)
gallon (gal)	264.2	cubic meter (m³)
cubic foot (ft³)	7.48	cubic meter (m³)
Flow rate		
gallon per minute (gal/min)	15.85	liter per second (L/s)

Temperature in degrees Celsius (°C) may be converted to degrees Fahrenheit (°F) as follows:

$$°F=(1.8×°C)+32$$

Temperature in degrees Fahrenheit (°F) may be converted to degrees Celsius (°C) as follows:

$$°C= (°F-32)/1.8$$

Datums

Vertical coordinate information is referenced to the North American Vertical Datum of 1988 (NAVD 88).

Horizontal coordinate information is referenced to North American Datum of 1983 (NAD 83).

Altitude, as used in this report, refers to distance above the North American Vertical Datum of 1988 (NAVD 88).

Water-Quality Units

Specific conductance is given in microsiemens per centimeter at 25 degrees Celsius (µS/cm at 25 °C).

Concentrations of chemical constituents in water are given either in milligrams per liter (mg/L) or micrograms per liter (µg/L).

Minimum reporting level (MRL)—Smallest measured concentration of a constituent that may be reliably reported by using a given analytical method (Timme, 1995).

Arsenic-Related Water Quality with Well Depth and Water Quality in Well-Head Samples from Production Wells, Oklahoma, 2008

By Carol J. Becker, S. Jerrod Smith, James R. Greer, and Kevin A. Smith

Abstract

The U.S. Geological Survey well profiler was used to describe arsenic-related water quality with well depth and identify zones yielding water with high arsenic concentrations in two production wells in central and western Oklahoma that yield water from the Permian-aged Garber-Wellington and Rush Springs aquifers, respectively. In addition, well-head samples were collected from 12 production wells yielding water with historically large concentrations of arsenic (greater than 10 micrograms per liter) from the Garber-Wellington aquifer, Rush Springs aquifer, and two minor aquifers: the Arbuckle-Timbered Hills aquifer in southern Oklahoma and a Permian-aged undefined aquifer in north-central Oklahoma.

Three depth-dependent samples from a production well in the Rush Springs aquifer had similar water-quality characteristics to the well-head sample and did not show any substantial changes with depth. However, slightly larger arsenic concentrations in the two deepest depth-dependent samples indicate the zones yielding noncompliant arsenic concentrations are below the shallowest sampled depth.

Five depth-dependent samples from a production well in the Garber-Wellington aquifer showed increases in arsenic concentrations with depth. Well-bore travel-time information and water-quality data from depth-dependent and well-head samples showed that most arsenic contaminated water (about 63 percent) was entering the borehole from perforations adjacent to or below the shroud that overlaid the pump.

Arsenic concentrations ranged from 10.4 to 124 micrograms per liter in 11 of the 12 production wells sampled at the well head, exceeding the maximum contaminant level of 10 micrograms per liter for drinking water. pH values of the 12 well-head samples ranged from 6.9 to 9. Seven production wells in the Garber-Wellington aquifer had the largest arsenic concentrations ranging from 18.5 to 124 micrograms per liter. Large arsenic concentrations (10.4–18.5) and near neutral to slightly alkaline pH values (6.9–7.4) were detected in samples from one well in the Garber-Wellington aquifer, three production wells in the Rush Springs aquifer, and one well in an undefined Permian-aged aquifer. All well-head samples were oxic and arsenate was the only species of arsenic in water from 10 of the 12 production wells sampled. Arsenite was measured above the laboratory reporting level in water from a production well in the Garber-Wellington aquifer and was the only arsenic species measured in water from the Arbuckle-Timbered Hills aquifer.

Fluoride and uranium were the only trace elements, other than arsenic, that exceeded the maximum contaminant level for drinking water in well-head samples collected for the study. Uranium concentrations in four production wells in the Garber-Wellington aquifer ranged from 30.2 to 99 micrograms per liter exceeding the maximum contaminant level of 30 micrograms per liter for drinking water. Water from these four wells also had the largest arsenic concentrations measured in the study ranging from 30 to 124 micrograms per liter.

Introduction

Arsenic is a known carcinogen (World Health Organization, 2001), and ingestion of inorganic arsenic, of which 30–90 percent may be supplied by drinking water, is believed to cause bladder, kidney, lung, and liver cancer in humans (Smith and others, 1992). The risk of an individual dying from arsenic-related cancers as a result of lifetime ingestion of water with arsenic concentration at 50 micrograms per liter (μg/L) could be as great as 13 in 1,000 (Smith and others, 1992). To address this risk, the U.S. Environmental Protection Agency (EPA) in 2000 reduced the maximum contaminant level (MCL) for arsenic in drinking water from public water-supply systems from 50 to 10 μg/L (U.S. Environmental Protection Agency, 2001). The new arsenic rule became enforceable on January 23, 2006, affecting many municipalities and water districts in the United States, especially those in the West, Midwest, and Northeast (Welch and others, 2000). As many as 23 public water-supply systems in Oklahoma have been affected by the reduced arsenic MCL of 10 μg/L for drinking water (J. Craig, Director Water Quality Division, Oklahoma Department of Environmental Quality, written commun., 2005). Most large communities in Oklahoma are financially able to address noncompliant drinking water. Unfortunately, many small communities and rural water districts operate with small resources, maintain minimal conveyance infrastructure, and often have no secondary source of water.

Selection of appropriate rehabilitation strategies for an individual well requires information about the heterogeneity and interconnectedness of aquifer materials, well construction details, especially the method of well completion, and, most valuably, changes in flow contribution and water quality with depth in the well. Wireline velocity logs and packer tests are the traditional methods for collecting depth-dependent flow and water-quality data, however these methods do not always provide representative information about aquifer characteristics during production and are time consuming, invasive, and expensive.

A combined well-bore travel time and depth-dependent water sampler (Izbicki and others, 1999), referred to as the U.S. Geological Survey (USGS) well profiler, has been used by USGS investigators to evaluate well-bore travel time and collect samples at varying depths in a pumping well (Izbicki and others, 2008; Smith and others, 2009). The USGS well-profiler method provides many technical advantages such as less operating down time, minimal modification to the well, and also can be considerably less expensive than traditional methods of data collection. In terms of data quality, the most important advantage is that all data collection is performed while the well is pumping.

A project was performed by the USGS, in cooperation with the Oklahoma Department of Environmental Quality and the Groundwater Protection Council, to describe arsenic-related water quality with depth in two wells. The project used the USGS well profiler to determine if zones yielding water with high arsenic concentrations could be identified. The role of the Groundwater Protection Council in this project was to describe and evaluate the geohydrology of the aquifers studied and incorporate the geochemical results from the USGS well profiler into a generalized decision tree for identifying appropriate well-rehabilitation techniques. If the results showed that large arsenic concentrations in the borehole were related to stratigraphic zones or sedimentary layering, the USGS technique could be considered an option for identifying well-rehabilitation strategies that are less expensive than drilling new production wells or water treatment at the well head.

An additional objective was to collect well-head samples from production wells producing arsenic contaminated water. These data could then be used to better define the spatial distribution of arsenic and the geochemical processes controlling the presence of arsenic in selected aquifers.

Purpose and Scope

This report presents the results of an investigation that used the USGS well profiler to describe arsenic-related water quality with depth in two production wells in an attempt to identify zones yielding water with high arsenic concentrations.

This report also describes groundwater quality of well-head samples from 12 production wells in arsenic-affected aquifers.

The USGS well profiler was used on two production wells in central and western Oklahoma that yield water from the Garber-Wellington aquifer (GW) and the Rush Springs aquifer (RS), respectively. Groundwater samples were collected at the well head from 12 production wells (fig. 1 and table 1) yielding water from the GW, RS, and two minor aquifers, the Arbuckle-Timbered Hills aquifer (TH) in southern Oklahoma and a Permian-aged undefined aquifer (PM) in north-central Oklahoma.

Groundwater samples collected with the well profiler and at the well head were analyzed for the dissolved major ions and trace elements including the arsenic species; arsenite, arsenate, dimethylarsinate (DMA), monomethylarsonate (MMA), and total arsenic shown on table 2. Selected water properties—specific conductance, pH, water temperature, dissolved oxygen, and alkalinity also were measured (table 2). In this report, unless otherwise noted, the word arsenic refers to dissolved arsenic regardless of oxidation state.

Acknowledgments

The authors would like to thank Robert Pistole, Steve Ray, and Keith Wright for their willingness to assist and cooperation on this project. Gratitude also is expressed to the managers and well operators of the communities who graciously allowed USGS personnel to access and sample their production wells. Appreciation is extended to Mark Hildebrand and David Pruitt with the Oklahoma Department of Environmental Quality and Jim Roberts, Mike Nickolaus, and Mike Paque with the Ground Water Protection Council. Stan Paxton and William Andrews of the USGS Oklahoma Water Science Center and Christina Stamos-Pfeiffer of the USGS California Water Science Center provided suggestions for improving the manuscript.

Study Aquifers

The rock units most widely used as aquifers for drinking-water supply in central and western Oklahoma are the Garber Sandstone and the Rush Springs Formation (Christenson, 1998). These rock units and other Permian-aged rock units exposed at the surface in central and western Oklahoma are commonly referred to as "redbeds" because of the pronounced red color from iron oxide coatings on the mineral grain surfaces. Arsenic and the association with iron oxide and the geochemical processes controlling the adsorption and release of arsenic in the Garber Sandstone unit of the Garber-Wellington aquifer were studied extensively by the USGS National Water Quality Assessment (NAWQA) program. However, arsenic in other aquifers in Oklahoma, with regard to the source and related geochemical processes, has not been investigated.

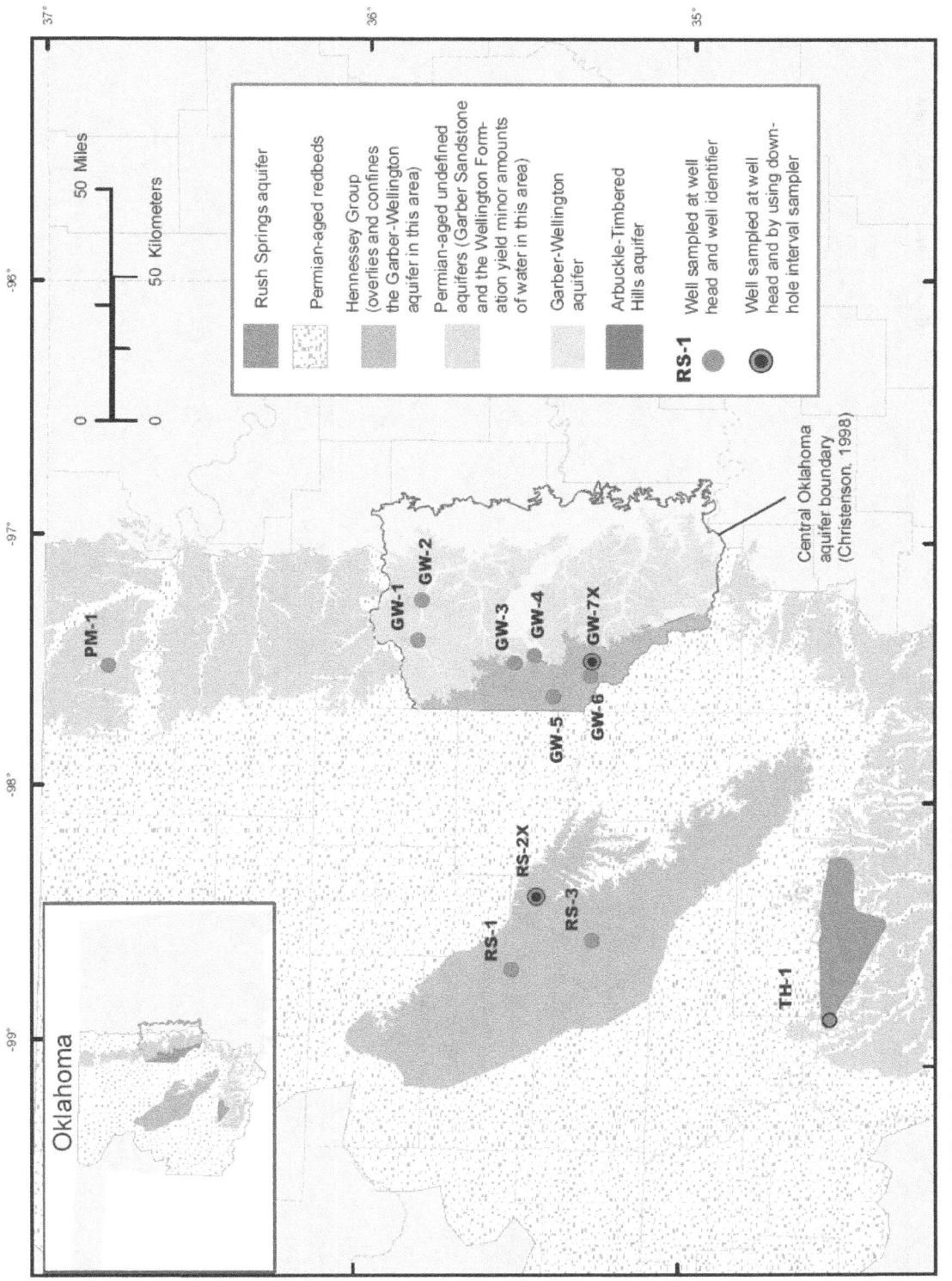

Base from U.S. Geological Survey digital data, 1:100,000, 1983
A bers Equal Area Conic projection, North American Datum 1983

Figure 1.   Location of production wells sampled and study aquifers, Oklahoma, 2008.

Table 1. Site and completion information for production wells sampled for arsenic in depth-dependent and well-head samples, Oklahoma, 2008.

[USGS, U.S. Geological Survey; ID, identifier; --, not available; lds, land surface; slotted, well casing is slotted near bottom of well; open, well is completed with no casing below surface casing; perforated, casing is perforated at selected zones]

USGS site ID	Well ID	Aquifer	Sample location	Land surface altitude[1] (feet)	Well depth (feet below lds)	Pump depth (feet below lds)	Static water level (feet below lds)	Pumping water level (feet below lds)	Completion type
352934097271502	GW-1	Garber-Wellington	well head	1,105	--[2]	--	--	--	slotted
355034097145201	GW-2	Garber-Wellington	well head	1,015	310	--	--	--	slotted
353308097290701	GW-3	Garber-Wellington	well head	1,120	750	683	--	--	perforated
352934097271502	GW-4	Garber-Wellington	well head	1,245	265	--	--	--	slotted
352604097370901	GW-5	Garber-Wellington	well head	1,233	854	680	--	--	perforated
351914097320201	GW-6	Garber-Wellington	well head	1,285	782	760	--	--	perforated
351853097284701	GW-7X	Garber-Wellington	well head; depth dependent	1,210	811	732	402	521	perforated
364824097311601	PM-1	Permian-aged undefined	well head	1,091	120	100	--	--	slotted
353237098403901	RS-1	Rush Springs	well head	1,638	320	260	--	--	open
352822098233801	RS-2X	Rush Springs	well head; depth dependent	1,676	294	270	169	220	open
351754098331501	RS-3	Rush Springs	well head	1,521	375	260	--	--	open
343706098451201	TH-1	Arbuckle Timbered Hills	well head	1,365	620	595	--	--	perforated

[1] Distance above North American Vertical Datum of 1988.

[2] Probably less than 300 feet below land surface based on a comparison to wells within a radius of 1.5 miles.

Table 2. Analysis methodologies, method references, and highest minimum reporting levels of water properties and chemical constituents measured in depth-dependant and well-head water samples from production wells, Oklahoma, 2008. All constituents are dissolved unless otherwise noted.

[US EPA, U.S. Environmental Protection Agency; μS/cm, microsiemens per centimeter; °C, degree Celsius; --, not applicable; mg/L, milligram per liter; μg/L, microgram per liter; $CaCO_3$, calcium carbonate]

Water properties and chemical constituents (units)	Maximum contaminant level (US EPA, 2009)	Secondary maximum contaminant level (US EPA, 2009)	Method references	Highest minimum reporting level
Oxygen, field, (mg/L)	--	--	Wilde and Radtke (1998)	0.1
pH, field, (standard units)	--	6.5 to 8.5	Wilde and Radtke (1998)	.1 standard units
Specific conductance, field, (μS/cm at 25 °C)	--	--	Wilde and Radtke (1998)	3 significant digits
Water temperature, field, (°C)	--	--	Wilde and Radtke (1998)	.5
Calcium, (mg/L)	--	--	Fishman (1993)	.02
Magnesium, (mg/L)	--	--	Fishman (1993)	.012
Potassium, (mg/L)	--	--	Fishman and Friedman (1989)	.06
Sodium, (mg/L)	--	--	Fishman (1993)	.12
Alkalinity, field, (mg/L as $CaCO_3$)	--	--	Rounds and Wilde (2001)	3 significant digits
Bicarbonate, field, (mg/L)	--	--	Rounds and Wilde (2001)	3 significant digits
Carbonate, field, (mg/L)	--	--	Rounds and Wilde (2001)	3 significant digits
Bromide, (μg/L)	--	--	Fishman and Friedman (1989)	.02
Chloride, (mg/L)	--	250	Fishman and Friedman (1989)	.12
Fluoride, (mg/L)	4	2	Fishman and Friedman (1989)	.08
Silica, (mg/L)	--	--	Fishman (1993)	.02
Sulfate, (mg/L)	--	250	Fishman and Friedman (1989)	.18
Dissolved solids, total, (mg/L)	--	500	Fishman and Friedman (1989)	3 significant digits
Aluminum, (μg/L)	--	50 to 200	Garbarino and others (2006)	4
Antimony, (μg/L)	6	--	Garbarino and others (2006)	.14
Arsenate, (μg/L)	--	--	Garbarino and others (2002)	.8
Arsenic, (μg/L)	10	--	Garbarino and others (2006)	.06
Arsenic, total, (μg/L)	10	--	Garbarino and others (2006)	.2
Arsenite, (μg/L)	--	--	Garbarino and others (2002)	1.2
Dimethylarsinate, (μg/L)	--	--	Garbarino and others (2002)	.6
Monomethylarsonate, (μg/L)	--	--	Garbarino and others (2002)	1.8
Barium, (μg/L)	2,000	--	Garbarino and others (2006)	.4
Beryllium, (μg/L)	4	--	Garbarino and others (2006)	.02
Boron, (μg/L)	--	--	Garbarino and others (2006); Garbarino (1999)	4
Cadmium, (μg/L)	5	--	Garbarino and others (2006)	.04
Chromium, (μg/L)	100	--	Garbarino and others (2006)	.12
Cobalt, (μg/L)	--	--	Garbarino and others (2006)	.02

Table 2. Analysis methodologies, method references, and highest minimum reporting levels of water properties and chemical constituents measured in depth-dependant and well-head water samples from production wells, Oklahoma, 2008. All constituents are dissolved unless otherwise noted—Continued.

Water properties and chemical constituents (units)	Maximum contaminant level (US EPA, 2009)	Secondary maximum contaminant level (US EPA, 2009)	Method references	Highest minimum reporting level
Copper, (µg/L)	[1]1,300	1,000	Garbarino and others (2006)	1
Iron, (µg/L)	--	300	Fishman (1993)	8
Lead, (µg/L)	[1]15	--	Garbarino and others (2006)	.06
Lithium, (µg/L)	--	--	Garbarino and others (2006); Garbarino (1999)	1
Manganese, (µg/L)	--	50	Garbarino and others (2006)	.2
Molybdenum, (µg/L)	--	--	Garbarino and others (2006)	.02
Nickel, (µg/L)	--	--	Garbarino and others (2006)	.20
Selenium, (µg/L)	50	--	Garbarino and others (2006)	.04
Silver, (µg/L)	--	100	Garbarino and others (2006)	.1
Strontium, (µg/L)	--	--	Garbarino (1999); Garbarino and others (2006)	.8
Uranium, (µg/L)	30	--	Garbarino and others (2006)	.006
Vanadium, (µg/L)	--	--	Garbarino and others (2006)	.16
Zinc, (µg/L)	--	5,000	Garbarino and others (2006)	2

[1] Copper and lead are regulated by a treatment technique that requires systems to control the corrosiveness of the water. If more than 10 percent of tap water samples exceed the maximum contaminant level, water systems must take corrective steps. For copper, the action level is 1,300 µg/L, and for lead is 15 µg/L (US EPA, 2009).

Rush Springs Aquifer

The Rush Springs aquifer (RS) is equivalent to the Rush Springs Formation in west-central Oklahoma (fig. 2). The aquifer is generally less than 250-foot thick and composed of very fine-grained to fine-grained sandstone with interbedded dolomite or gypsum (Becker and Runkle, 1998). Sand grains composing the Rush Springs Formation in Caddo County are loosely cemented with iron oxide and calcite (Tanaka and Davis, 1963). Overlying the aquifer in the western part are beds of massive gypsum interbedded with shale and siltstone. Well yields from the Rush Springs aquifer vary depending on location and depth. Well yields generally are high in the aquifer with most irrigation wells producing more than 1,000 gallons per minute (gpm) (Becker and Runkle, 1998).

Permian-Aged Undefined Aquifer

In north-central Oklahoma, groundwater is produced from minor aquifers that consist of intermittent layers of permeable sandstone and limestone in rocks that are predominantly composed of shale (Beldon, 1997). The Garber

Sandstone and Wellington Formation make up more than half of the rock units in this part of the state, but are not considered a major source of groundwater because of the high percentage of shale (Beldon, 1997). Groundwater from the Permian-aged rock units in this area is calcium magnesium-bicarbonate water type with dissolved solids ranging from 500 to 2,000 mg/L (Bingham and Bergman, 1980).

Garber-Wellington Aquifer

The Garber-Wellington aquifer (GW) is composed of the Garber Sandstone and the Wellington Formation and together these two formations yield the greatest quantities of usable water in central Oklahoma (fig. 1 and fig. 2). Both formations are part of a larger aquifer system, used for domestic and public supply, referred to as the Central Oklahoma aquifer (COA). The rock units that compose the COA, including the Garber Sandstone and the Wellington Formation, extend north and southwest, but typically are not used for drinking-water supply beyond the COA boundaries because of inadequate yields.

System	Stratigraphic unit			Aquifer	
Permian	Whitehorse Group		Rush Springs Formation	Rush Springs aquifer (RS)	Central Oklahoma aquifer (Christenson, 1998)
			Marlow Formation		
	El Reno Group		Dog Creek Shale		
			Blaine Gypsum		
	Hennessey Group		Salt Plains Formation		
			Fairmont Shale		
	Sumner Group		Garber Sandstone	Garber-Wellington aquifer (GW); undefined aquifers in north-central Oklahoma (PM)	
			Wellington Formation		
	Chase, Council Grove, and Admire Groups, undivided				

System	Stratigraphic unit		Aquifer
Ordovician	Upper part of Arbuckle Group	Upper part of Arbuckle Group undifferentiated	Arbuckle-Timbered Hills aquifer (TH)
		West Spring Creek Formation and Kindblade Formation	
		Cool Creek Formation and McKenzie Hill Formation	
Cambrian	Lower part of Arbuckle Group and Timbered Hills Group	Signal Mountain Formation	
		Royer Dolomite Fort Sill Limestone	
		Honey Creek Formation	
		Reagan Sandstone	

Figure 2. Geologic units and equivalent aquifer units.

The hydrogeology of the GW has been studied and described at length by Parkhurst and others (1996), Christenson and others (1992), Christenson (1998), and Harrington and Roberts (2005). In brief, the total thickness of the Garber Sandstone and Wellington Formation ranges from 1,100 to 1,600 feet (ft) (Christenson and others, 1992) and consists of stacked channel bars, floodplain deposits, and related fluvial facies (Stanley Paxton, U.S. Geological Survey, written commun., 2005) that grade into one another vertically and horizontally.

Most domestic, stock, and irrigation wells in the aquifer draw water from less than 300 ft below land surface. Most public-supply wells, however, bypass the shallow aquifer system and produce water from greater than 300 ft below land surface. Deep wells that tap the confined aquifer system in the western one-quarter of the COA, where the GW is overlain by the Hennessey Group, are more likely to exceed the arsenic MCL than wells in the unconfined part of the aquifer (Schlottmann and others, 1998). Schlottmann and others (1998) estimated that about 30 percent of deep wells in the confined GW produced water with arsenic concentrations exceeding 50 μg/L, and only 2.4 percent of deep wells in the unconfined aquifer system produced water with arsenic concentrations exceeding 50 μg/L.

The geochemistry of trace elements in the COA, including arsenic, was studied by the USGS NAWQA program in detail. Schlottman and others (1998) showed that arsenic in the Garber Sandstone is adsorbed onto iron oxide probably in the form of goethite and hematite coatings on mineral surfaces. The highest percentage of arsenic and iron are contained by the clays in the Garber Sandstone and decreases with an increase in mineral grain size (Gromadzki, 2004). The clays have a high cation-exchange capacity, permitting sodium ions in the clays to exchange with calcium and magnesium ions in the water (Parkhurst and others, 1996). During the exchange, the water becomes undersaturated with respect to dolomite and in response, more dolomite dissolves and more calcium and magnesium are available for cation exchange (Parkhurst and others, 1996). As cation exchange and dolomite dissolution continue at depth, the pH gradually increases (Parkhurst and others, 1996) and at a pH value of 8.5, arsenic begins to desorb from the iron oxide coatings (Schlottmann and others, 1998). In general, cation exchange between water and clay minerals in the Garber Sandstone becomes more prevalent as water becomes older with depth. These conditions are most frequently found where the Garber Sandstone is confined by the Hennessey Group (Christenson, 1998). The confined conditions tend to cause this part of the aquifer to be poorly flushed by fresh water and as a result the water has a longer residence time and has been altered by cation exchange to a greater degree (Schlottman and others, 1998). As a consequence, large arsenic concentrations in this part of the aquifer are characteristically associated with sodium-rich water types and high pH values.

Arbuckle-Timbered Hills Aquifer

The Arbuckle-Timbered Hills aquifer (TH) is considered a minor aquifer in Oklahoma because of limited areal extent and the small number of wells completed in the aquifer. The aquifer is composed of a thick sequence of Cambrian- to Ordovician-aged limestone, dolomite, sandy dolomite, mudstone, conglomerate, and shale about 6,000 ft thick (Havens, 1977). Wells completed in the TH produce groundwater from solution openings, fractures, and faults in the limestone and dolomite sections in the aquifer. Groundwater is of sodium-bicarbonate and sodium-chloride type with some sulfate (Havens, 1983). Fluoride concentrations are elevated in the TH and usually exceed the EPA MCL of 4 milligrams per liter (mg/L) in drinking water (Havens, 1983).

Geochemical Processes Affecting Arsenic Concentrations in Groundwater

Sources of arsenic in groundwater can be anthropogenic or naturally occurring. Anthropogenic sources include abandoned mines and mine waste, agricultural pesticides, and wood preservatives. Naturally occurring sources of arsenic include geothermal waters, oxidation of arsenic sulfide minerals, and arsenic adsorbed onto iron oxides, aluminum oxides, and clay minerals (Welch and others, 2000; Sracek and others, 2004).

Arsenic in groundwater is commonly in two oxidation states: arsenite and arsenate. Arsenite, the most toxic of the arsenic species, is 4 to 10 times more soluble than arsenate and most likely to be in groundwater during reducing conditions (U.S. Environmental Protection Agency, 2002). Arsenate is most prevalent in oxygenated water at neutral and alkaline pH values. Both arsenic species adsorb onto a variety of metal oxides. However, iron oxide is the most adsorbent substrate because of chemistry and prevalence of iron oxide throughout the hydrogeologic environment (Hinkle and Polette, 1998), especially in Oklahoma aquifers.

Geochemical processes affecting the desorption of arsenic from iron oxides are pH of the water, structural changes of crystalline iron oxide, and dissimilatory iron reduction (Welch and others, 2000). Arsenate adsorbs to iron oxide in neutral and lower pH water but desorbs as pH values become alkaline. Because the pH increases, the surface charge of the iron oxide becomes negative and repels arsenate and other negatively charged ions that compete for adsorption sites (Sracek and others, 2004; Kresse and Fazio, 2003). Desorption of arsenic from iron oxide has been shown as the largest source of arsenic to water in other aquifers throughout the United States (Robertson, 1989; Welch and others, 2000). Desorption of arsenic also happens during the conversion of crystalline iron oxide to other mineral phases. Changes in the crystalline structure can decrease the number of adsorption sites releasing arsenic and other ions (Hinkle and Polette, 1998; Fuller and others, 1993). Desorption of arsenic from iron oxide also results from the biologically mediated process of dissimilatory iron reduction, which happens in reducing environments with large amounts of decaying organic matter. During those conditions, bacteria cause arsenic as arsenite to desorb from available iron oxide into groundwater (Stollenwerk, 2003). The organoarsenicals DMA and MMA also are found in groundwater during these conditions, being biologically mediated forms of arsenic indicative of reducing conditions.

Methods of Study

The USGS well profiler was used to describe changes in water quality with depth in two production wells; RS-2X

in the RS and GW-7X in the GW. Tracer-pulse travel-time profiles were constructed to determine appropriate depths for depth-dependent sampling between zones contributing flow. Tracer-pulse travel-time profiles are shown on graphs (figs. 3 and 4) and the zones sampled are shown on plots with measured concentrations of arsenic and selected major ions (figs. 5 and 6).

Water samples were collected at the well head from 12 production wells: GW-1 through GW-6 and GW-7X in the GW; PM-1 in the PM; RS-1, RS-3, and RS-2X in the RS; and TH-1 in the TH (fig. 1 and table 1). The water-quality data were grouped by water type and by aquifer to study relations between arsenic and the other trace elements. Percentages of the major-ion concentrations, in milliequivalents, were used to determine water type and to construct Piper diagrams (Piper, 1944) to illustrate water-quality characteristics and common trends in water quality. Cations and anions were considered dominant when composing 50 percent or more of the total ion concentration expressed in milliequivalents per liter. Ions were considered to be secondary when composing between 25 and 49 percent of the total ion concentration.

U.S. Geological Survey Well Profiler

Candidate Well Selection

The RS-2X and GW-7X production wells were selected from a list of candidate production wells with arsenic concentrations exceeding the MCL of 10 µg/L and by using criteria that were considered necessary to facilitate safe and efficient access to the well:

- The ability of the community to manage water-supply needs without the use of the well during the testing period.

- A minimum 10-inch diameter cased or open borehole with greater than 2 inches of clearance between the production pipe and borehole wall or casing.

- A minimum 1.5-inch diameter access port at the well head that allows direct vertical access inside the casing.

- A sampling port in the production line (preferably at the well head) that allows collection of representative samples of produced water.

- A blow-off valve that allows produced water to be discharged at the surface without entering the distribution system.

Some additional criteria that were not necessary to facilitate access to the production wells by using the USGS well profiler, but were considered to increase the likelihood of sampling success were:

- A 1.25-inch diameter slotted polyvinylchloride (PVC) access tube attached to the pump column.

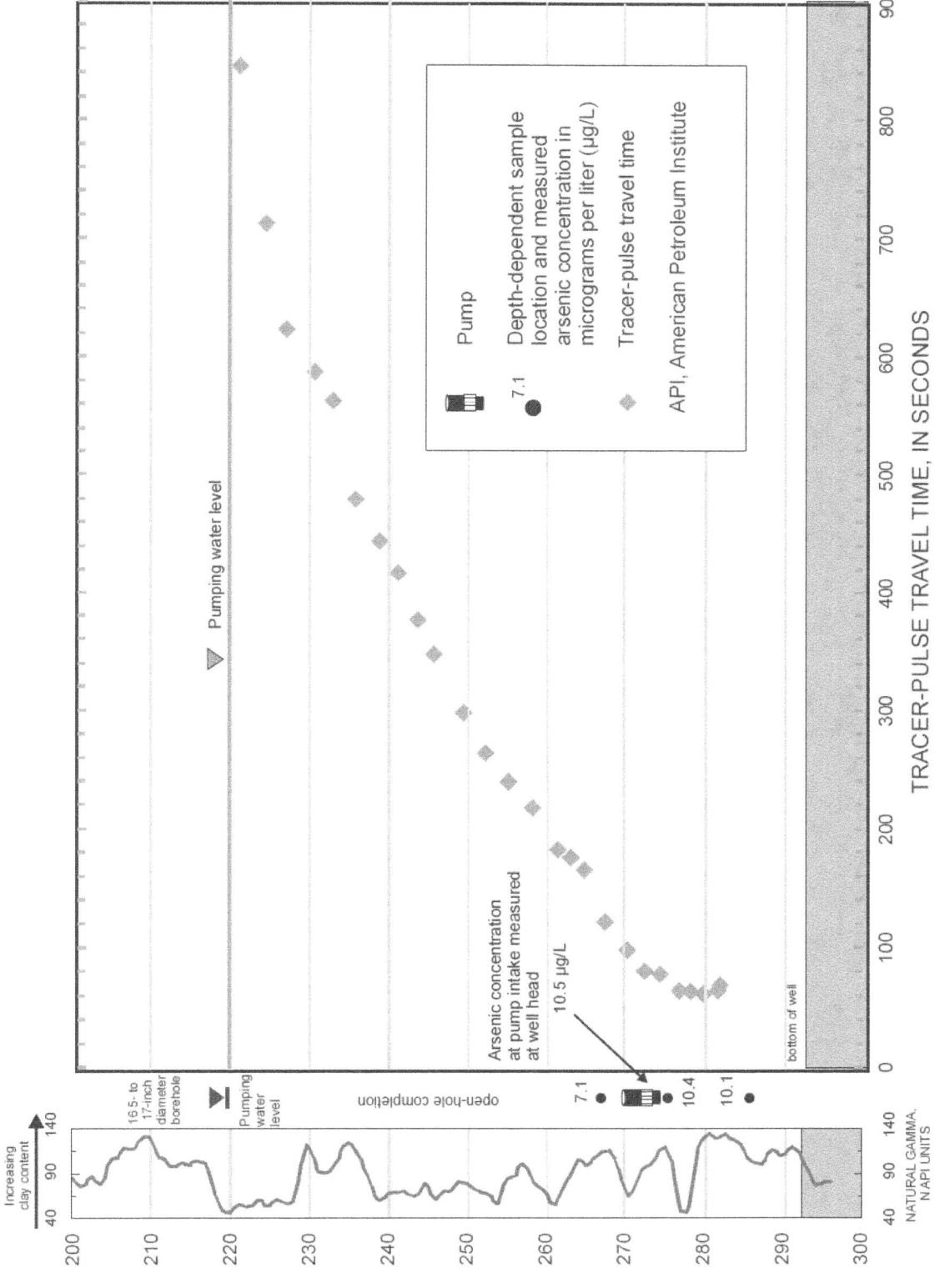

Figure 3. Estimated tracer-pulse travel times, depth-dependent sample locations, and well construction information for production well RS-2X in the Rush Springs aquifer, Oklahoma, 2008.

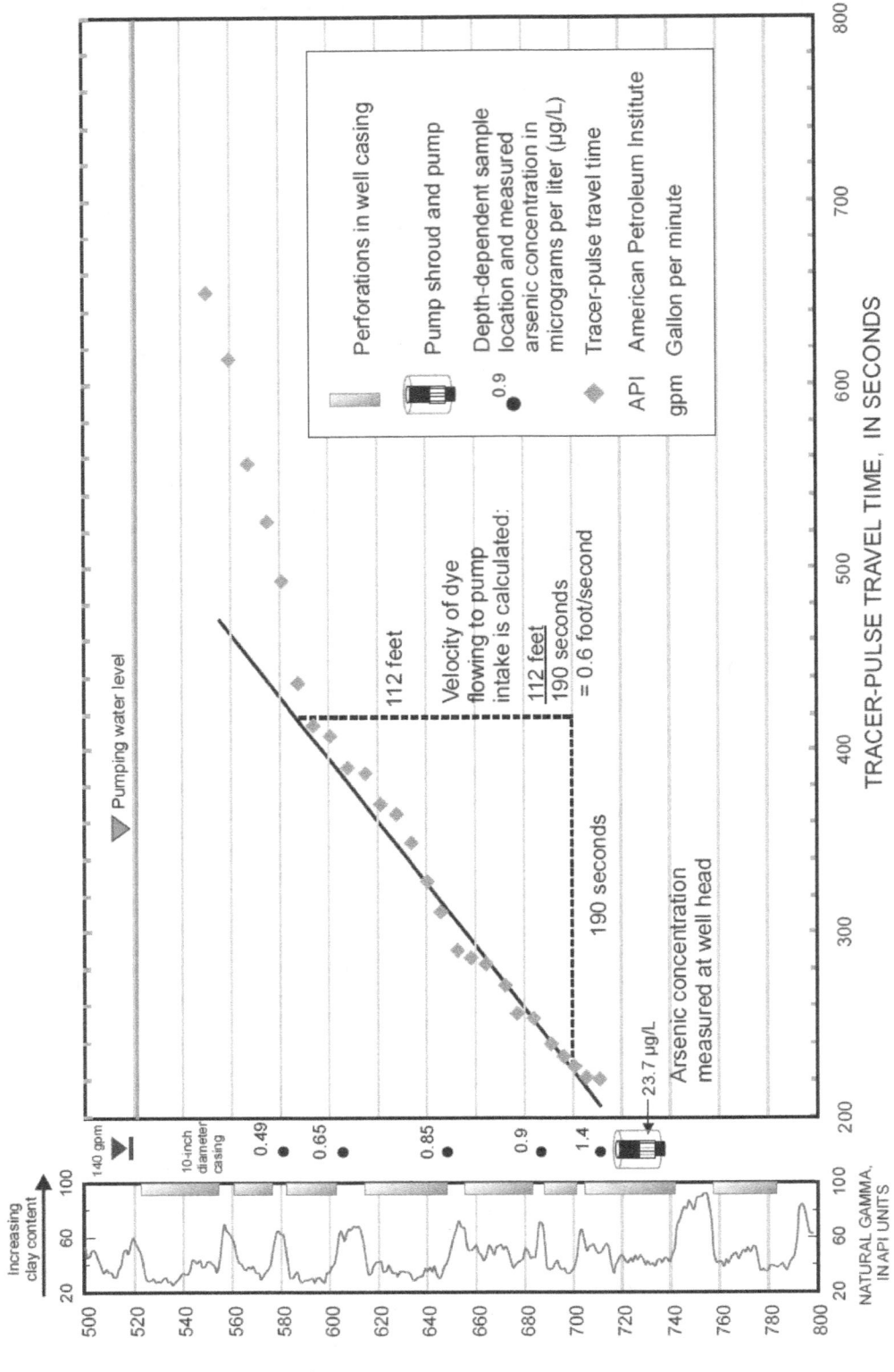

Figure 4. Estimated tracer-pulse travel times, depth-dependent sample locations, and well construction information for production well GW-7X in the Garber-Wellington aquifer, Oklahoma, 2008.

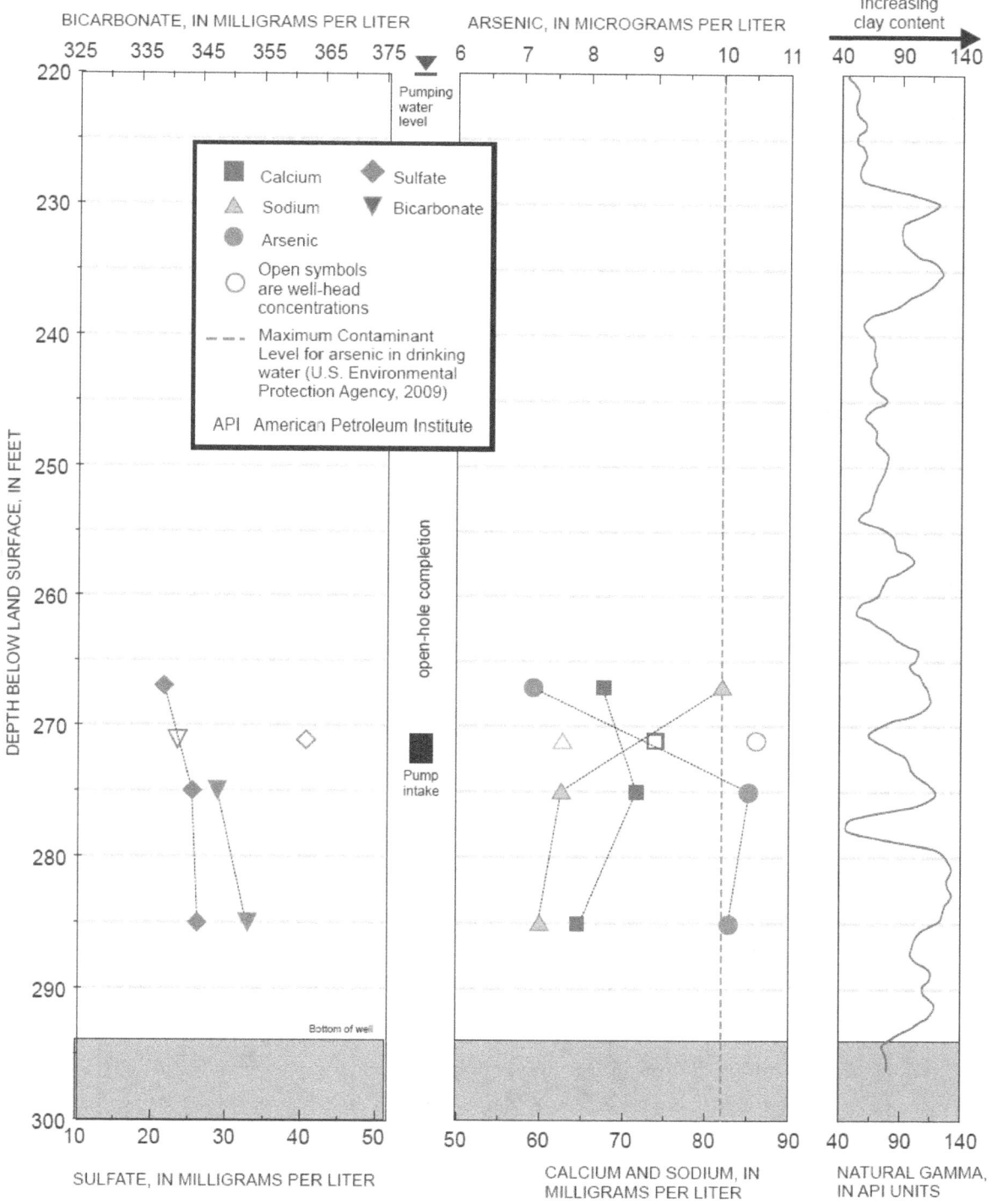

Figure 5. Concentrations of arsenic, bicarbonate, calcium, sodium, and sulfate in depth-dependent samples and well-head sample from production well RS-2X in the Rush Springs aquifer, Oklahoma, 2008.

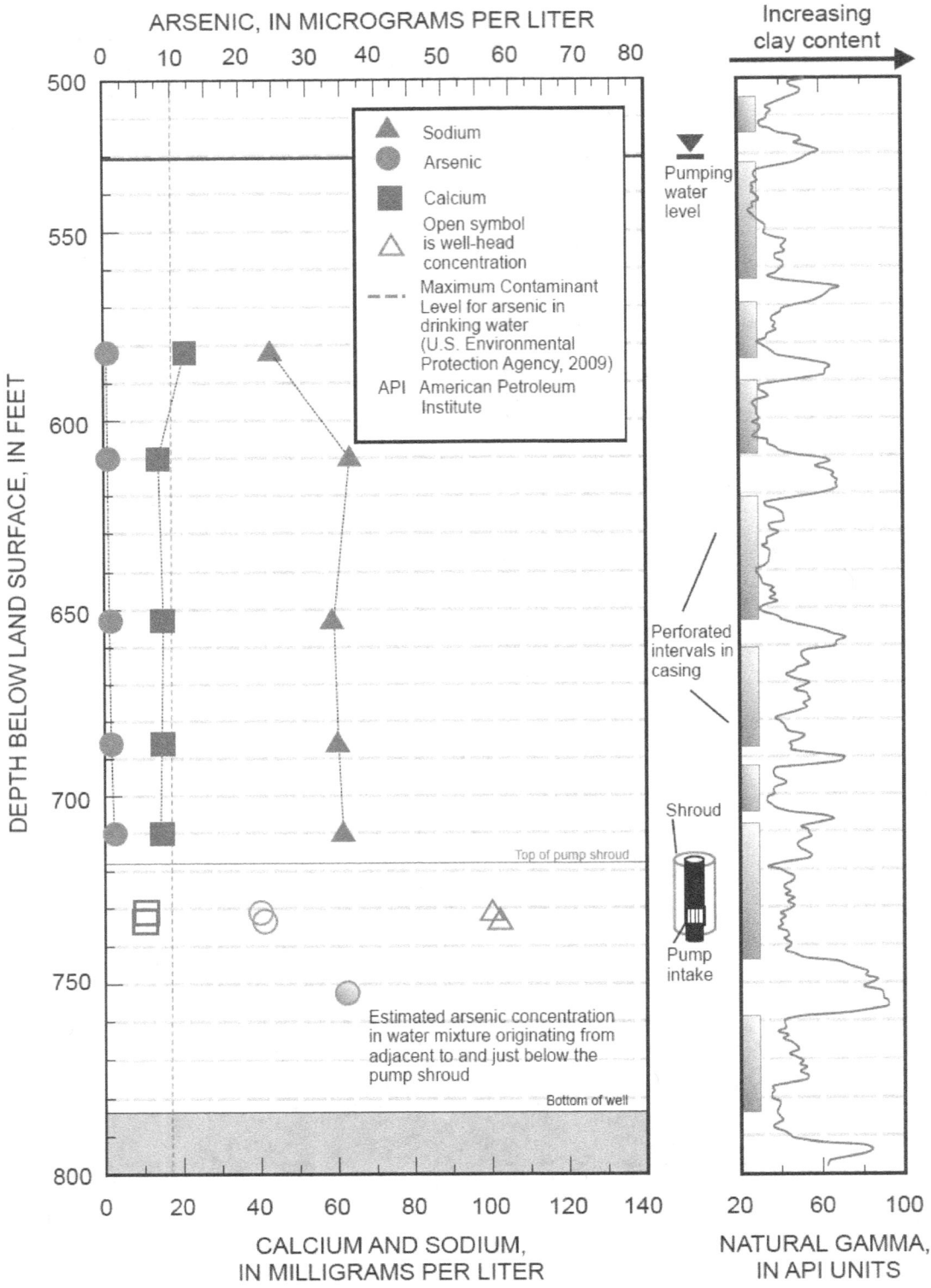

Figure 6. Concentrations of arsenic, calcium, and sodium in depth-dependent samples and well-head samples from production well GW-7X in the Garber-Wellington aquifer, Oklahoma, 2008.

- A submersible pump set high in the well rather than lower.

- The production well must be able to pump continuously for 10 hours per day for as many as 5 days.

Geophysical Logs

Prior to depth-dependent sampling the RS-2X well, the down-hole pump and production casing were removed from the non-cased hole and a gamma-ray dual-induction caliper logging tool was run by Hayes Evaluation Logging and Perforating from Anadarko, Oklahoma. The gamma-ray is used as an indicator of rock lithology and was used to determine boundaries between the sandstones and clayey zones in the borehole. In general, clays have a larger content of radioactive materials whereas sandstones have smaller amounts of clay and can be identified as having low natural gamma radiation (Keys, 2005a). This type of log is commonly used in perforated well completions after the casing has been set to locate water producing sandstones for perforation. The dual-induction log is used to measure the resistivity of the formation, which provides information about the pore fluids and porosity of the rocks. This information is also used to determine boundaries between rock layers (Keys, 2005b). The caliper log provides a continuous measure of the borehole diameter and also provides information about rock lithology and fracturing (Keys, 2005c).

After the geophysical log had been run, the pump and production casing were put back into the hole and tracer-pulse travel times were collected. Zones having higher sand content and less clay were identified on the geophysical logs, this information along with the travel-time information were used to identify the depths or stratigraphic zones contributing water to the well for depth-dependent sampling.

The GW-7X well had an existing geophysical log (gamma-ray neutron) with casing perforations provided by the well operator. The geophysical log had been run after the well originally was drilled and cased to locate stratigraphic zones having high sand/low clay content for perforating. The travel-time information and the geophysical log were used to identify the depths for depth-dependent sampling.

Dye Tracer-Pulse Travel-Time Profile

To obtain tracer-pulse travel-time data, the well profiler used a slim, high-pressure, multipurpose hose filled with a dilute, nontoxic, rhodamine-dye tracer solution. Figure 7 shows a generalized diagram of a perforated production well, similar to GW-7X, showing the well profiler and deployment of the hose into the pumping well. The hose was lowered as deep as possible and a small amount of the tracer solution was injected into the water column. The hose was subsequently raised several feet and another pulse of tracer solution was injected into the well. The tracer pulse travels to the pump intake at the same velocity as water traveling in the well borehole or casing. A small part of the well-head discharge

from the pumping well was routed through a field fluorometer (Turner Designs model 10-AU), which reports the tracer concentration (in micrograms per liter) at one-second intervals. The difference in time between tracer injection and detection at the surface was recorded as the travel time in seconds for the given depth. The travel times were plotted in relation to well depth and combined with ancillary information, such as well diameter, the following were concluded: (1) depth of the pump intake (minimum travel time), (2) changes in water velocities in the well, (3) estimated depths of contributing intervals, and (4) the pumping water level.

Depth-Dependent Sampling

After contributing intervals were identified, the well-profiler hose was drained of tracer solution and a stainless-steel-reinforced Teflon sample hose was attached to the end of the multipurpose hose. A check valve separated the two hoses and prevented contamination of the sample hose by residual tracer solution. A second check valve was attached to the other end of the sample hose and both hoses were pressurized with compressed nitrogen gas. When a sample depth was reached, samples were collected by opening the manual valve on the surface end of the hose. When the hose depressurized, the hydrostatic pressure of the water column in the well exceeded the pressure inside the hose. The in-line check valves opened and sample water filled the hose to about the pumping water level. The manual valve at the surface was closed and the water-filled hose was reeled to the surface. The pressure of the water column inside the hose was great enough to close the in-line check valves during hose retrieval. The sample hose was 50 ft in length and contained a storage volume of about 0.33 gallon. Once at the surface, the sample-hose attachment (including check valves) was disconnected from the multipurpose hose and compressed nitrogen was used to force the sample water out of the sample hose through plastic tubing and a filter into polyethylene bottles. To completely fill the sample hose and obtain enough water to fill sample bottles, the end of the sample hose had to be at least 50 ft below the pumping water level.

An enclosed chamber was used to prevent wind-borne contamination of the sampled water. Trace elements samples were preserved by acidification to a pH of 2 or less by using 2 milliliters of nitric acid. The arsenic speciation sample was preserved by acidification with 100 microliters of ethylenediaminetetraacetic acid (EDTA).

Each sample collected with the well profiler represented conditions at a discrete depth in the pumping well, not a specific hydrogeologic zone in the formation. The sample was a mixture of water from several contributing zones, with the number of zones represented in the mixture increasing in the direction of the pump. Without reliable estimates of zonal production, a mass-balance approach could not be used to estimate constituent concentrations from each zone. As a result, the depth-dependent water-quality data were only used to draw qualitative comparisons between zones.

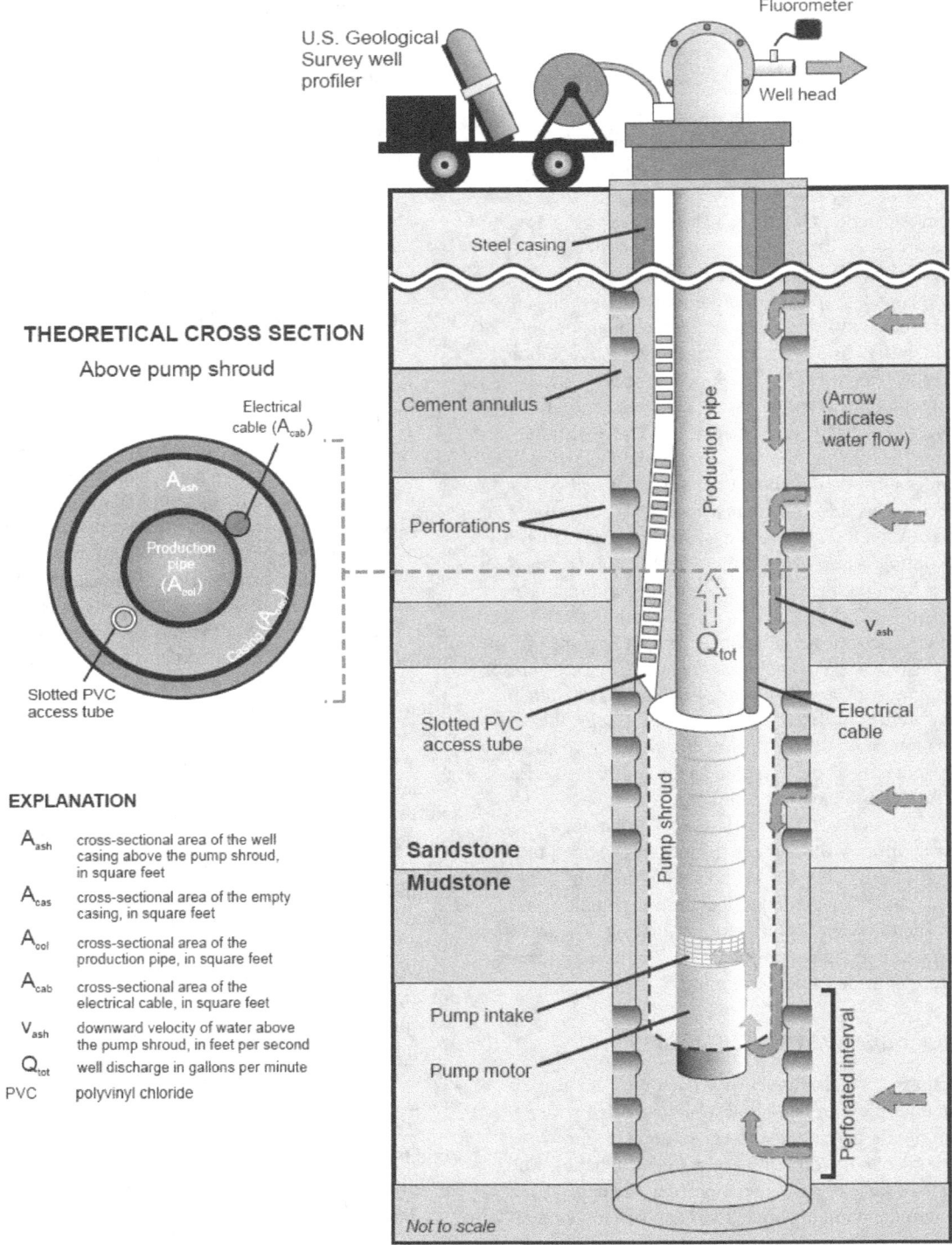

U.S. Geological Survey well profiler

Fluorometer

Well head

Steel casing

THEORETICAL CROSS SECTION

Above pump shroud

Electrical cable (A_{cab})

A_{ash}

Production pipe (A_{col})

Casing (A_{cas})

Slotted PVC access tube

Cement annulus

Perforations

(Arrow indicates water flow)

Production pipe

Q_{tot}

V_{ash}

Slotted PVC access tube

Electrical cable

Pump shroud

Sandstone

Mudstone

Pump intake

Pump motor

Perforated interval

Not to scale

EXPLANATION

A_{ash} cross-sectional area of the well casing above the pump shroud, in square feet

A_{cas} cross-sectional area of the empty casing, in square feet

A_{col} cross-sectional area of the production pipe, in square feet

A_{cab} cross-sectional area of the electrical cable, in square feet

V_{ash} downward velocity of water above the pump shroud, in feet per second

Q_{tot} well discharge in gallons per minute

PVC   polyvinyl chloride

Figure 7.   Diagram of perforated well GW-7X showing well construction, deployment of the U.S. Geological Survey well profiler, and the theoretical horizontal well cross section just above the pump shroud.

Laboratory Analysis

All samples were processed by using established USGS protocols described in Wilde and others (2004). Water properties of the depth-dependent samples were measured in a YSI XL multiprobe meter cup and recorded after there was less than a 10-percent variation in specific conductance and less than 0.2-unit variation in pH (appendix 1). Dissolved oxygen and water temperature were recorded but were not necessarily representative of the water in the aquifer. Alkalinity, bicarbonate, and carbonate concentrations were measured by using an inflection point titration method described by Rounds and Wilde (2001). Water samples were analyzed at the USGS National Water Quality Laboratory in Denver, Colorado, for dissolved concentrations of the major ions, trace elements, and arsenic species shown on table 2.

Quality-Assurance Procedures

Laboratory decontamination of sampling equipment was performed by using USGS standard methods (Wilde, 2004). The same procedures were applied to sample hoses and fittings with one exception. The sample-hose attachment is Teflon-lined and would normally be rinsed with a 5-percent hydrochloric-acid solution. This step was not applied because the acid rinse would damage the permanently attached stainless-steel fittings.

Quality-control samples for samples collected by using the well profiler consisted of one replicate and an equipment blank. A replicate sample is an extra sample set collected with the environmental sample to determine the accuracy of laboratory analytical procedures.

The analytical accuracy between the environmental and replicate samples collected by the depth dependent sampler was computed as the relative percent difference (RPD) of constituent concentrations by using the following equation:

$$RPD = [(C1-C2) / ((C1+C2)/2)] * 100$$

Where;
- C1 = larger of the two concentrations
- C2 = smaller of the two concentrations

Relative percent difference values were not calculated if one constituent had an estimated concentration or a concentration less than the minimum reporting level.

The RPD values for major ions measured in the depth-dependent samples (well RS-2X) ranged from 0 to 19 percent and for trace elements the RPD values ranged from 0 to 150 percent (appendix 2). The RPD value for arsenic was 0.

Large RPD values can result from sequential and not simultaneous collection of environmental and replicate samples. Large RPD values also can be caused by small concentrations reported with few significant figures. For example, concentrations of 2 and 3 would give an RPD of 40 percent; whereas, if the concentrations were reported with more significant figures, such as 2.4 and 2.6, the RPD would be 8 percent.

An equipment blank was collected to determine if samples were contaminated by the sampling equipment or bottles. An equipment blank sample showed contamination of calcium, fluoride, silica, aluminum, barium, copper, lead, nickel, silica, and zinc (appendix 2). The only constituents measured at elevated concentrations of importance in the blank sample were copper, lead, and zinc. Concentrations of these trace elements in the equipment blank sample were larger than concentrations measured in the depth-dependent samples from GW-7X.

Well-Head Sampling of Production Wells

The 12 production wells were operating and purged before sampling. All wells were sampled from a garden-hose spigot on the well head by using a length of plastic tubing with a polypropylene adaptor that screwed onto the spigot. The water properties specific conductance, pH, temperature, and dissolved oxygen were measured every 5-7 minutes during the purging process by using a flow-through chamber with an YSI multi-probe meter. The meter calibrations were performed every morning before use. The specific conductance and pH calibrations used standard solutions that bracketed the expected values. Samples were collected after water properties had stabilized during the purging process. The criteria for stabilization were less than a 10-percent variation in specific conductance, less than 0.2-unit variation in pH, and less than 0.3-mg/L variation in dissolved oxygen. Filtered water was collected in polyethylene bottles in an enclosed sampling chamber to prevent wind-borne contamination. Trace elements samples were preserved by acidification to a pH of 2 or less by using 2 milliliters of nitric acid. The arsenic speciation sample was preserved by acidification with 100 microliters of ethylenediaminetetraacetic acid (EDTA).

Laboratory Analysis

Well-head samples were analyzed for dissolved concentrations of the major ions, trace elements, and arsenic species shown on table 2. Alkalinity, bicarbonate, and carbonate concentrations were measured by using an inflection point titration method described by Rounds and Wilde (2001).

Water-quality samples were collected and processed by using established USGS protocols described in U.S. Geological Survey (2006) and Wilde and others (2004). Samples were shipped on ice over night to the USGS National Water Quality Laboratory in Denver, Colorado.

Quality-Assurance Procedures

Equipment for well-head sampling was cleaned at the USGS Oklahoma Water Science Center by using a nonphosphate detergent, plastic brush, and peristaltic pump, and rinsed with tap water followed by deionized water. Equipment was then rinsed with an acid solution consisting of 5 percent hydrochloric acid and rinsed again with deionized water. Equipment was air dried, then wrapped in new plastic bags and used one time between each cleaning.

Quality-control samples for well-head sampling consisted of one replicate and a matrix spike for arsenate, arsenite, DMA, and MMA. Two replicates were collected; however one was lost in shipment. The analytical accuracy between the environmental and replicate sample collected at the well head was computed as the RPD of constituent concentrations. The RPD values for major ions measured in water from well-head samples from GW-3 ranged from 0 to 6.9 percent and for trace elements measured in well-head samples, the RPD values ranged from 0 to 20 percent. The RPD value for arsenic was 2.1 percent (appendix 2).

The matrix spike is a quality-control sample used to evaluate the effects of the sample-water chemistry on the performance of the laboratory-analytical method (Sandstrom and Lewis, 2009). Three samples were collected from well GW-3 on August 7, 2008; an environmental sample, a replicate, and a third sample that was spiked with 20 µg/L each of arsenate, arsenite, DMA, and MMA. Arsenic concentrations in the environmental and replicate samples from GW-3 were about 4.7 µg/L. The measured concentrations of arsenite, DMA, and MMA in the spiked sample each should have been 20 µg/L and arsenate around 24.7 µg/L. The measured concentrations in the spiked sample were arsenate 31.5 µg/L, arsenite 17.5 µg/L, DMA 22.1 µg/L, and MMA 21.9 µg/L.

Arsenic-Related Water Quality with Well Depth

Production Well RS-2X in the Rush Springs Aquifer

The RS-2X production well was selected for sampling with the well profiler based on the selection criteria and that it had historical arsenic concentrations averaging around 10 µg/L (Keith Wright, City of Hinton, Oklahoma, personal commun., 2008). A well-head sample collected prior to this study in 2008 by USGS personnel had a total arsenic concentration of 11.4 µg/L.

Well Construction and Sampling Conditions

The RS-2X production well was cased from land surface to about 20 ft with 16.5- to 17-inch diameter surface casing (fig. 3). Below 20 ft, the well was open hole in sandstone and finer-grained sediments down to a total depth of 294 ft. The borehole averaged about 16.5 to 17 inches in diameter to a depth of 254 ft where the formation was washed out and the

diameter increased to about 21 inches. The well had a 5-ft long submersible pump that was set at 270 ft below land surface. The static water level was 169 ft below land surface and the pumping water level was 220 ft below land surface. Prior to sampling, the production pipe and submersible pump were temporarily removed from the borehole and natural gamma dual-induction caliper log was run.

Water Quality with Depth

Three intervals contributing flow were selected for sampling on the basis of the tracer-pulse travel-time profile, the natural gamma log curve, and the completion information shown on figure 3. Aided by this information, three depth-dependent samples were collected at 267 ft, 275 ft, and 285 ft. There were no samples collected below 285 ft because of entanglement of the well-profiler hose with electrical wiring on the production casing.

The well-head sample collected from the RS-2X production well had an arsenic concentration of 10.5 µg/L, a dissolved oxygen concentration of 9.2 mg/L, and a near neutral pH of 7.2 (appendix 1). Arsenic concentrations in the depth-dependant samples ranged from 7.1 to 10.4 µg/L with pH values ranging from 7.2 to 7.4 (table 3). Dissolved oxygen concentrations ranged from 7 to 15.4 mg/L (appendix 1) in the depth-dependent samples but probably were not accurate because of exposure to air.

The Piper diagram (Piper, 1944) on figure 8 illustrates that the well-head and depth-dependent samples have similar water-quality characteristics by the close proximity of the sample points on the plot and does not show any apparent water-quality trends with depth. Constituent concentrations that varied between the well-head and depth-dependent samples were arsenic, sodium, and sulfate. The shallow depth-dependent sample (267 ft) had the smallest arsenic and largest sodium concentrations compared to the well-head and the two deeper samples (275 and 285 ft) (fig. 5) and may indicate that zones yielding noncompliant arsenic concentrations are below 267 ft.

The sulfate concentration was about two times greater in the well-head sample, 41.2 mg/L, than the depth-dependent samples collected above and below the pump. The reason for the discrepancies in sodium, sulfate, and arsenic in samples is unknown. Water with elevated sulfate concentrations may have entered the well from the zone (269–272 ft) adjacent to the pump intake (fig. 5). During production, this water would travel horizontally to the pump intake and not be captured in depth-dependent samples from above and below the pump intake. However, more samples would be needed below the pump to better define any water-quality trends with depth and locate where arsenic-contaminated water is entering the borehole. This additional information may help determine whether zonal isolation would be a feasible option to lower arsenic concentrations in this well.

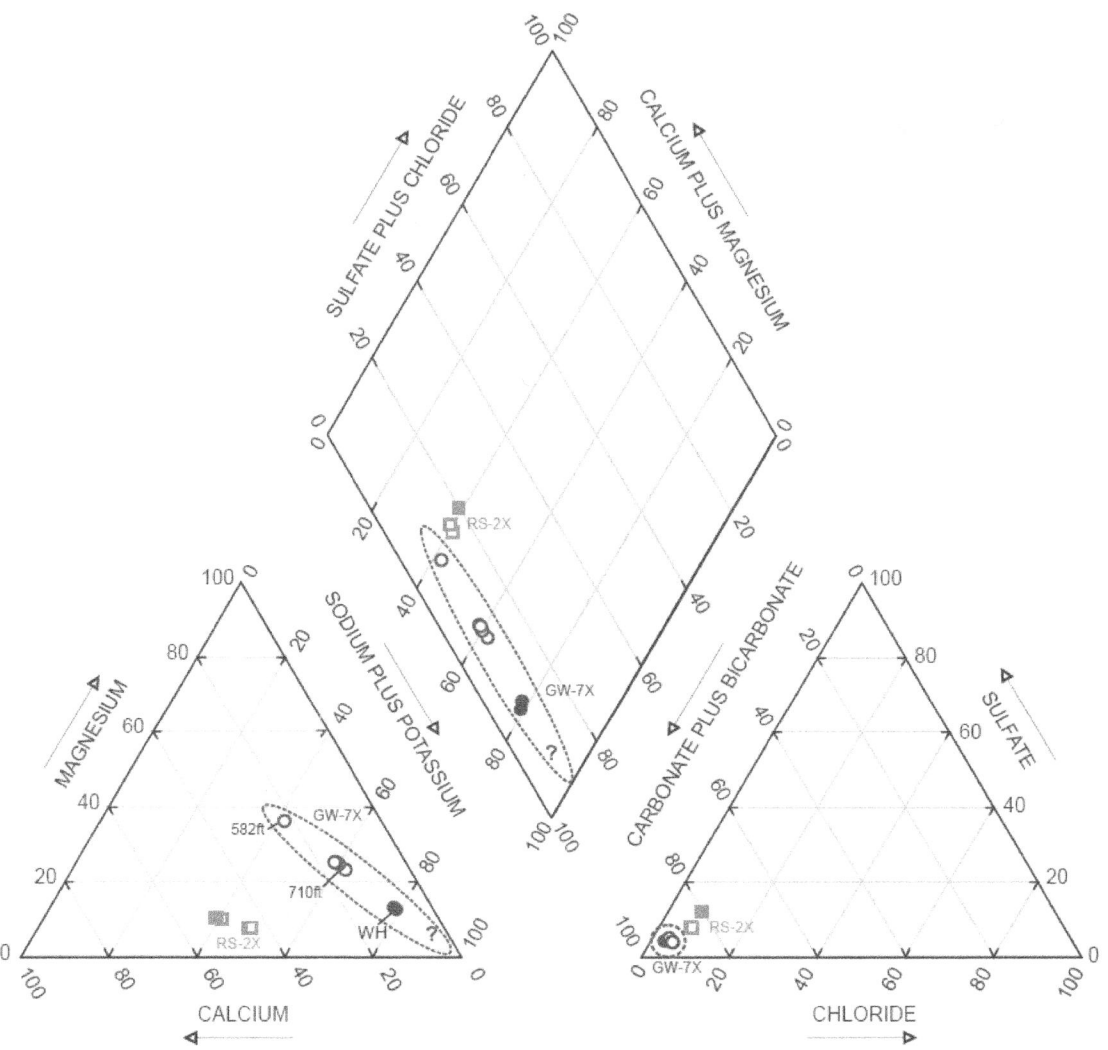

Percentage of total milliequivalents per liter

EXPLANATION

⬭   Outline of trend showing cation exchange process in samples from the GW-7X production well

▦   Well-head sample from RS-2X in the Rush Springs aquifer
☐   Depth-dependent sample from RS-2X in the Rush Springs aquifer (the 267-foot sample did not have a bicarbonate measurement and is absent in the right (anion) triangle

●   Well-head sample from GW-7X in the Garber-Wellington aquifer
○   Depth-dependent sample from GW-7X in the Garber-Wellington aquifer

?   Probable composition of water originating from adjacent to and below the pump shroud in GW-7X (based on wells with similar construction and water quality with depth S.J. Smith, written commun., 2009)

Figure 8. Percentages of major ions in well-head and depth-dependent samples from production wells GW-7X in the Garber-Wellington aquifer and RS-2X in the Rush Springs aquifer, Oklahoma, 2008.

Table 3.   Sample location, water type, pH, and arsenic concentration of water from depth-dependent and well-head samples from production wells, Oklahoma, 2008.

[μg/L, micrograms per liter; --, not available; ID, identifier; lds, land surface]

Well ID	Aquifer	Sample location (feet below lds)	Water type	pH (standard units)	Arsenic dissolved (μg/L)
GW-1	Garber-Wellington	well head	sodium bicarbonate	8.8	30
GW-2	Garber-Wellington	well head	sodium bicarbonate	7.8	124
GW-3	Garber-Wellington	well head	sodium-magnesium bicarbonate-chloride	8.0	4.8
GW-4	Garber-Wellington	well head	sodium-calcium bicarbonate	7.1	18.5
GW-5	Garber-Wellington	well head	sodium bicarbonate	8.5	59.9
GW-6	Garber-Wellington	well head	sodium bicarbonate-chloride	8.6	37.7
GW-7X	Garber-Wellington	well head before depth-dependent samples	sodium bicarbonate	8.7	22.9
GW-7X	Garber-Wellington	582	sodium-magnesium bicarbonate	7.8	.49
GW-7X	Garber-Wellington	610	sodium bicarbonate	8.0	.65
GW-7X	Garber-Wellington	653	sodium-magnesium bicarbonate	8.2	.85
GW-7X	Garber-Wellington	686	sodium bicarbonate	8.1	.9
GW-7X	Garber-Wellington	710	sodium bicarbonate	8.1	1.4
GW-7X	Garber-Wellington	well head after depth-dependent samples	sodium bicarbonate	8.7	23.7
PM-1	Permian-aged undefined	well head	calcium-sodium bicarbonate-chloride	6.9	10.4
RS-1	Rush Springs	well head	calcium-sulfate bicarbonate	7.4	18.2
RS-2X	Rush Springs	well head	calcium-sodium bicarbonate	7.2	10.5
RS-2X	Rush Springs	267	--	7.4	7.1
RS-2X	Rush Springs	275	calcium-sodium bicarbonate	7.3	10.4
RS-2X	Rush Springs	285	calcium-sodium bicarbonate	7.2	10.1
RS-3	Rush Springs	well head	calcium bicarbonate	7.4	15.7
TH-1	Arbuckle Timbered Hills	well head	sodium bicarbonate	9.0	11.6

Production Well GW-7X in the Garber-Wellington Aquifer

The USGS well profiler was used to collect dye tracer-pulse travel-time information and five depth-dependent samples in the GW-7X production well in the GW. At the time of testing, the production well had been out of operation for 2.5 years because historical arsenic concentrations ranging from about 25 to 28 μg/L resulted in the well being noncompliant (Robert Pistole, Project Manager, Veolia Water North America, oral commun., 2008). The well was purged for about 72 hours before any samples were collected.

Well Construction and Sampling Conditions

The production well GW-7X was completed with casing that was perforated at intervals from 522 ft to the bottom of the well at 783 ft (Steve Ray, City of Moore, Oklahoma, written commun., 2009) (fig. 4). For this type of well completion, the casing is cemented to the formation borehole and perforations (opening through which water enters the well) are made through the casing and cement annulus at permeable aquifer zones, usually identified from a natural gamma geophysical log after the casing has been installed.

An 8-inch diameter PVC shroud overlaid the pump at 718 ft (fig. 6). The shroud is similar to an open-bottom tube that surrounds the submersible pump and forces water to flow past the motor to reach the pump intake, keeping the motor cool during production (Cheapa Pumps, 2009; Driscoll, 1986). The pump intake was about 14 ft below the top of the shroud at 732 ft with about 5 ft of pump motor extending below the pump intake. There was about 51 ft of formation below the bottom of the pump. The static water level was 402 ft below land surface before testing began and 521 ft below land surface while the well was pumping (fig. 6).

Obstructions and irregularities of the casing wall and pump column can impede the movement of the sampling hose into and out of the well. To circumvent potential problems, the pump column was pulled from the well and a 1.25-inch diameter, 0.375-inch slotted PVC access tube was installed to guide the sample hose down the borehole. The bottom end of the access tube was open, cut at an angle, and ended at the top of the shroud that was not removed for sampling (fig. 7). There was insufficient space between the shroud and casing to extend the PVC or well-profiler sample hose below the pump. As a result there were no tracer-pulse travel-time data or depth-dependent samples collected below the shroud.

Water Quality with Depth

In well GW-7X, five depths were selected for sampling on the basis of information obtained from the tracer-pulse travel-time profile and natural gamma log curve shown on figure 4. Two well-head samples were collected to measure arsenic concentrations, one before and another after the depth-dependent samples were collected to see if concentrations had changed in produced water with time. Depth-dependent samples were collected above the shroud at 582 ft, 610 ft, 653 ft, 686 ft, and 710 ft.

All samples from well GW-7X, well head and depth dependent, were oxic with dissolved oxygen ranging between 5.3 to 8.6 mg/L (appendix 1). However, measurements of dissolved oxygen in depth-dependent samples were probably not accurate because of exposure to air during sampling.

There was a distinct difference in pH values, major-ion composition, and arsenic concentrations between the depth-dependent and well-head samples from well GW-7X. Well-head samples showed higher pH values (appendix 1), smaller concentrations of calcium, and larger concentrations of arsenic and sodium than depth-dependent samples (fig. 6). pH values at the well head were 8.7, while pH values in depth-dependent samples ranged from 7.8 (582 ft) to 8.2 (653 ft) and increased with depth (table 3). Arsenic concentrations in well-head samples stayed relatively constant in produced water, ranging from 22.9 µg/L before testing and 23.7 µg/L after testing. Depth-dependent sample concentrations were substantially smaller, ranging from 0.49 µg/L (582 ft) to 1.4 µg/L (710 ft), and similar to pH, increased with depth. The oxic conditions and arsenate in all samples, indicated that pH-activated desorption from iron oxide coatings is most likely the source and mechanism for release of arsenic, which is consistent with the NAWQA study findings relating to arsenic in the COA (Christenson, 1998).

Water type of samples from GW-7X was sodium-bicarbonate except for samples from 582 ft and 653 ft, which had slightly larger percentages of magnesium and were sodium-magnesium bicarbonate. The percentages of sodium and calcium ions in the depth-dependent samples show an inverse relation; as the percentage of sodium ions increases with depth, the calcium ions decrease. This trend is shown on the Piper diagram on figure 8 and corresponds to the exchange of sodium ions in the clays with calcium ions in the water, which becomes more prevalent as the water becomes older with depth. The effects from cation exchange also are seen in the increase of pH values and arsenic concentrations with depth. In addition to sodium and arsenic, well-head samples also had markedly larger concentrations of boron, chromium, lead, molybdenum, selenium, vanadium, and uranium than depth-dependent samples (appendix 1). These findings, in addition to the other water quality discrepancies between the well-head and depth-dependent samples, indicate that noncompliant produced water was entering the borehole from perforations adjacent to or below the shroud (fig. 7). This conclusion was supported by the calculations shown in this section that estimate that about 63 percent of the water produced at the well head originated adjacent to or below the shroud. By using this estimate and the arsenic concentrations in the well-head samples and the sample collected just above the shroud (710 ft), the water mixture in the borehole below the shroud was estimated to have an arsenic concentration of 36 µg/L, in a probable range of 30 to 56 µg/L.

From the tracer-pulse travel time in figure 4, the maximum downward velocity of water flowing through the well just above the pump shroud was 0.6 foot per second (ft/sec). This velocity can be converted to a volumetric flow rate, by using the equation:

$$Q_{ash} = V_{ash} * A_{ash} * 60 \text{ seconds per minute} * 7.48 \text{ gallons per cubic foot}$$

where

Q_{ash} is the maximum flow rate of water above the shroud, in gallons per minute,

V_{ash} is the velocity of water above the pump shroud (0.6 foot per second; fig. 7), and

A_{ash} is the theoretical cross-sectional area of the well casing above the pump shroud in square feet (fig. 7).

The theoretical cross sectional area of the well casing above the pump shroud (A_{ash}) can be computed as the cross sectional area of the empty well casing (A_{cas}), minus the areas of the production pipe (A_{col}) and electrical cable to the pump motor (A_{cab}), by using the equation;

$$A_{ash} = A_{cas} - A_{col} - A_{cab}$$

where
A_{ash} is the cross-sectional area of the well casing above the pump shroud, in square feet,
A_{cas} is the cross sectional area of the empty well casing, in square feet,
A_{col} is the cross sectional area of the production pipe, in square feet, and
A_{cab} is the cross sectional area of the electrical cable, in square feet.

For well GW-7X, which has a 10-inch diameter casing, a 4.5-inch outside diameter production pipe with 5.5-inch outside diameter collars (at the pipe joints), and a 1.5-inch diameter electrical cable, the idealized cross-sectional area of the well casing above the pump shroud was about 0.4 ft² (fig. 7). However, because of turbulence, friction loss, well scale buildup, and eddies created around the many objects in the well, the effective cross-sectional area was probably less than 0.4 ft². Smith and others (2009), by using an empirical approach on wells of identical construction to GW-7X, estimated that the effective cross-sectional area of the well casing above the pump shroud can range from 0.14 to 0.36 ft², and was about 0.21 ft² on average. By using these estimates of effective cross-sectional area, the downward flow rate just above the pump shroud could range from 90.5 to 37.1 gallons per minute (gpm), with an average downward flow rate of 55.6 gpm. Given that the total discharge of the well was about 150 gpm (Steve Ray, City of Moore, Oklahoma, oral commun., 2009) this equates to a flow contribution range of 60.3 to 24.7 percent of the total well discharge, with an average of 37.1 percent of the total discharge coming from above the pump.

Given the well-head arsenic concentration (C_{wh}) of 22.9 µg/L and the arsenic concentration (C_{ash}) of 1.4 µg/L from the depth-dependent sample collected from just above the pump shroud (fig. 6), the arsenic concentration of the water mixture originating from the zones adjacent to and below the pump shroud (C_{bsh}) was estimated at 36 µg/L by using the equation:

$$C_{bsh} = C_{wh} - ((P_{ash})(C_{ash})) / P_{bsh}$$

where
C_{bsh} is the arsenic concentration, in micrograms per liter, of the water mixture originating from the zones adjacent to and below the pump shroud,
C_{wh} is the concentration of arsenic in water produced at the well head (22.9 in micrograms per liter),

C_{ash} is the concentration of arsenic in depth-dependent sample collected just above the shroud (1.4 in micrograms per liter),
P_{ash} is the percentage of the total well discharge that originates from zones adjacent to or below the pump shroud, and
P_{bsh} is the percentage of the total well discharge (150 gallons per minute) that originates from zones above the shroud.

Arsenic-Related Water Quality in Well-Head Samples

Most of the 12 production wells sampled had historical arsenic concentrations exceeding 10 µg/L, and except for production well GW-7X, were on line and used for water supply (fig. 1). The well-head sample collected from GW-7X before testing was used to describe the water quality from this well. The arsenate, arsenite, DMA, and MMA water sample from well GW-3 collected in August 2008 was compromised and was not used in the report. A partial sample analysis from this well with concentrations of these arsenic species (collected September 2008) was used with the measured physical properties and major ion concentrations from the August 2008 sample for comparison in the report.

Seven production wells produced water from the GW, three from the RS, one from the TH, and one from PM (fig. 1 and table 3). The production wells ranged in depth from 120 to 854 ft (table 1). Four production wells (GW-1, GW-2, GW-4, PM-1) had slotted casing at the bottom of the well similar to completion techniques used to construct domestic wells. To maximize the volume of produced water for this type of well completion, the annulus between the casing and formation is filled with sand from the bottom of the well to near land surface which permits groundwater to flow into the slotted casing from the full saturated thickness of the aquifer penetrated.

Five wells had perforated casing open to the formation at varying intervals (GW-3, GW-5, GW-6, GW-7X, TH-1). Three production wells in the RS (RS-1, RS-2X, and RS-3) had open-hole completions, a common well-completion method in the RS for domestic, irrigation, and public-supply wells. For this type of well completion, casing is not installed below surface casing which allows groundwater to move towards the pump from all water bearing zones in the borehole.

Arsenic in Relation to Physical Properties and Water Type

Arsenic concentrations in well-head samples were larger than 10 µg/L, except for GW-3 at 4.8 µg/L, and ranged from 10.4 to 124 µg/L (table 3). Six of the seven production wells in the GW had the largest arsenic concentrations ranging from 18.5 to 124 µg/L. Large arsenic concentrations (10.4–18.5) and near neutral to slightly alkaline pH values (6.9–7.4) were detected in samples from production wells in the RS (RS-1, RS-2X, RS-3) in addition to GW-4 in the GW and PM-1 in the PM (fig. 9 and table 3). Schlottmann and others (1998) reported arsenic is not mobile at pH values below 8.5 in the GW and the coincidence of low pH values and large arsenic concentrations may be due to water mixing in the borehole from multiple zones.

All well-head samples were oxic and arsenate was the only species of arsenic in water from 10 of the 12 production wells sampled. Arsenite was measured above the laboratory reporting level in water from GW-4 and was the only arsenic species measured in water from TH-1. Arsenite is generally present in water during reducing conditions. However, the dissolved oxygen concentration of the sample was 3.7 mg/L, indicating oxic conditions. This discrepancy might be the result of water mixing in the borehole or the introduction of air from the sampling process.

Most samples showed larger concentrations of dissolved arsenic than total arsenic, which was not anticipated, because total arsenic is a measure of the dissolved and undissolved forms. This discrepancy might be attributed to analytic error

or to the different analytical techniques used to measure total and dissolved arsenic (David Mueller, U.S. Geological Survey, written commun., 2009). The average difference between total and dissolved concentrations was only 0.5 percent and was considered in an acceptable range. The small difference between dissolved and total arsenic concentrations in well-head samples (and depth-dependant samples) indicates that arsenic was dissolved in groundwater and not associated with particulate material (appendix 1).

Sodium and bicarbonate were the predominant ions of all well-head samples from the GW. Magnesium and chloride were secondary ions in GW-3 and chloride was a secondary anion in GW-6. The Piper diagram on figure 10 shows that the percentages of calcium plus magnesium and sodium plus potassium in the GW samples plot along a trend similar to the depth-dependent samples from GW-7X on figure 8 indicating the transition from a calcium to a sodium dominated water type.

Unlike the GW where sodium was the dominant cation, calcium composed the greatest percentage of cations in water from the RS production wells (49 to 68 percent) with sodium a dominant secondary cation only in RS-2X. Sulfate was the dominant anion in RS-1 and bicarbonate the dominant anion in water from RS-2X and RS-3 (fig. 10). Arsenic concentrations in the three RS production wells ranged from 10.5 to 18.2 µg/L with near neutral to slightly alkaline pH values of 7.2 and 7.4 (table 3). The largest arsenic concentration, 18.2 µg/L from RS-1, was associated with calcium-sulfate bicarbonate type water.

Water from production well TH-1 was sodium-bicarbonate type with sodium composing almost 100 percent of the cations and bicarbonate 65 percent of the anions (fig. 10 and table 3). The total dissolved solids concentration of 511 mg/L and the pH value of 9.0 exceeded the secondary maximum contaminant level of 500 mg/L and a value 8.5, respectively, for drinking water (U.S. Environmental Protection Agency, 2009). Arsenic and fluoride were measured at concentrations of 11.6 µg/L and 7.44 mg/L, respectively, and exceeded the MCLs of 10 µg/L and 4 mg/L, respectively, for drinking water (U.S. Environmental Protection Agency, 2009).

Water from the production well PM-1 was calcium sodium-bicarbonate chloride type with calcium composing 43 percent and sodium 36 percent of the total cations in the water sample. Total dissolved solids were measured at a concentration of 937 mg/L and exceeded the secondary maximum contaminant level of 500 mg/L for drinking water (U.S. Environmental Protection Agency, 2009). Arsenic was measured at a concentration of 10.4 µg/L and exceeded the MCL for drinking water (U.S. Environmental Protection Agency, 2009).

Arsenic in Relation to Other Trace Elements

In the COA, Schlottmann and others (1998) generally found that high concentrations of arsenic occurred with chromium, selenium, and vanadium. Figures 11 and 12 show

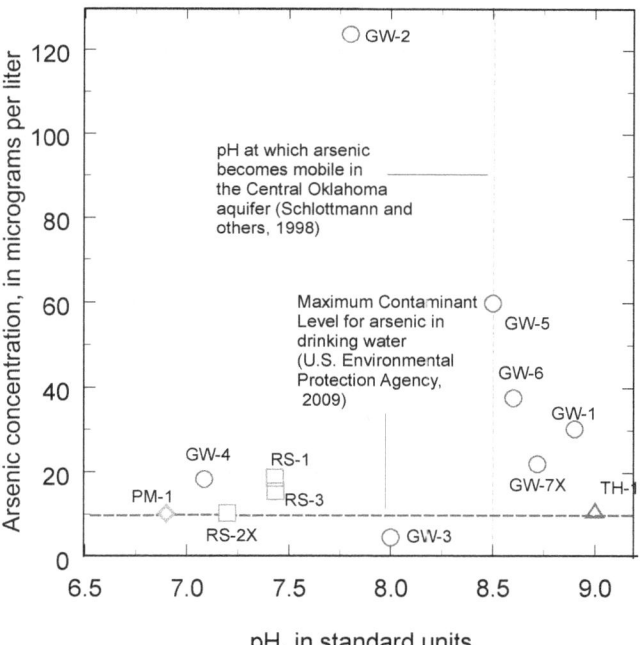

Figure 9. Relation of arsenic with pH in well-head samples from production wells, Oklahoma, 2008.

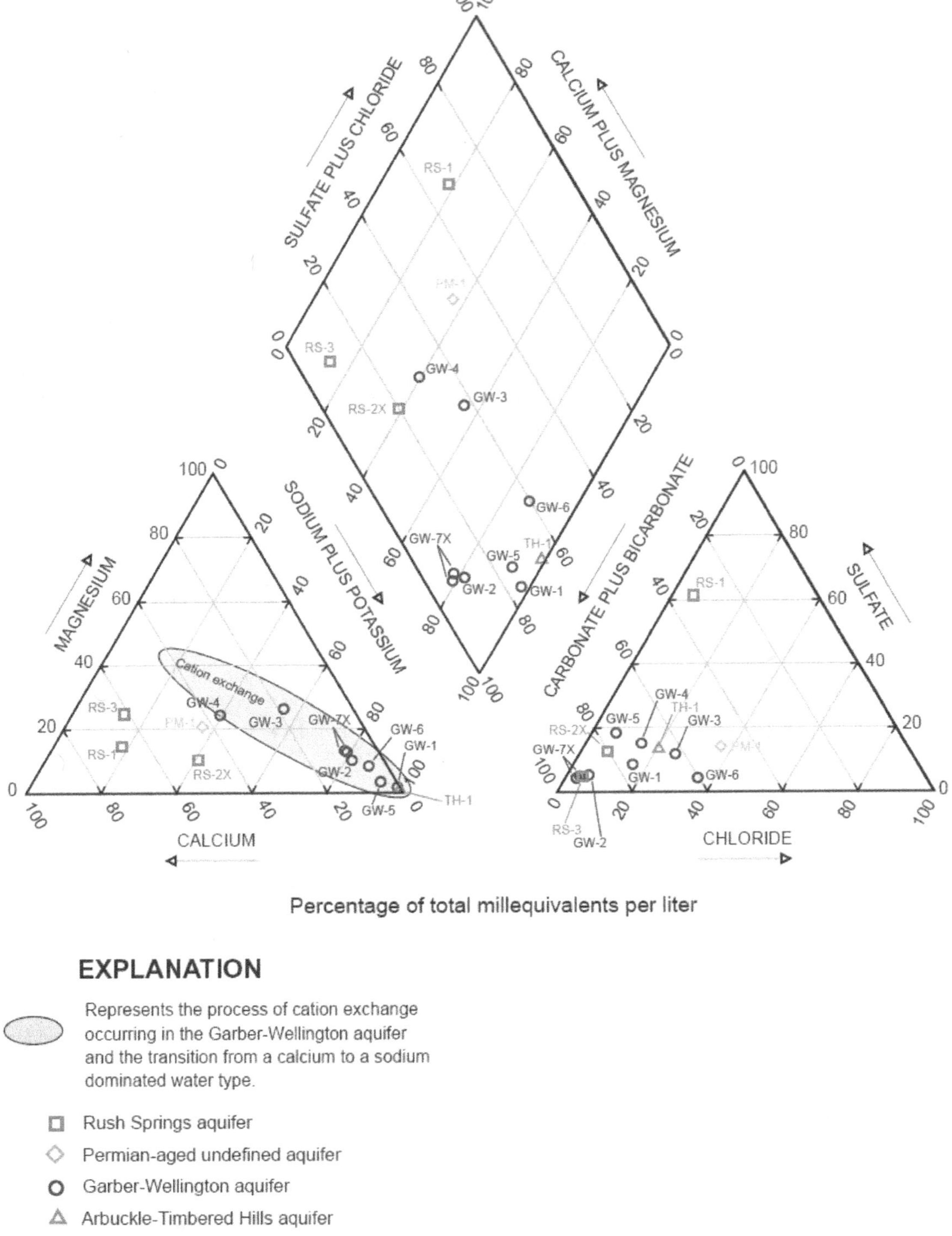

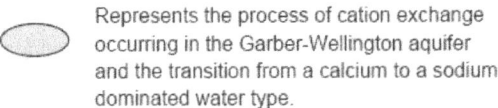

Percentage of total millequivalents per liter

EXPLANATION

Represents the process of cation exchange occurring in the Garber-Wellington aquifer and the transition from a calcium to a sodium dominated water type.

☐ Rush Springs aquifer

◇ Permian-aged undefined aquifer

○ Garber-Wellington aquifer

△ Arbuckle-Timbered Hills aquifer

Figure 10.   Percentages of major ions in well-head samples from production wells, Oklahoma, 2008.

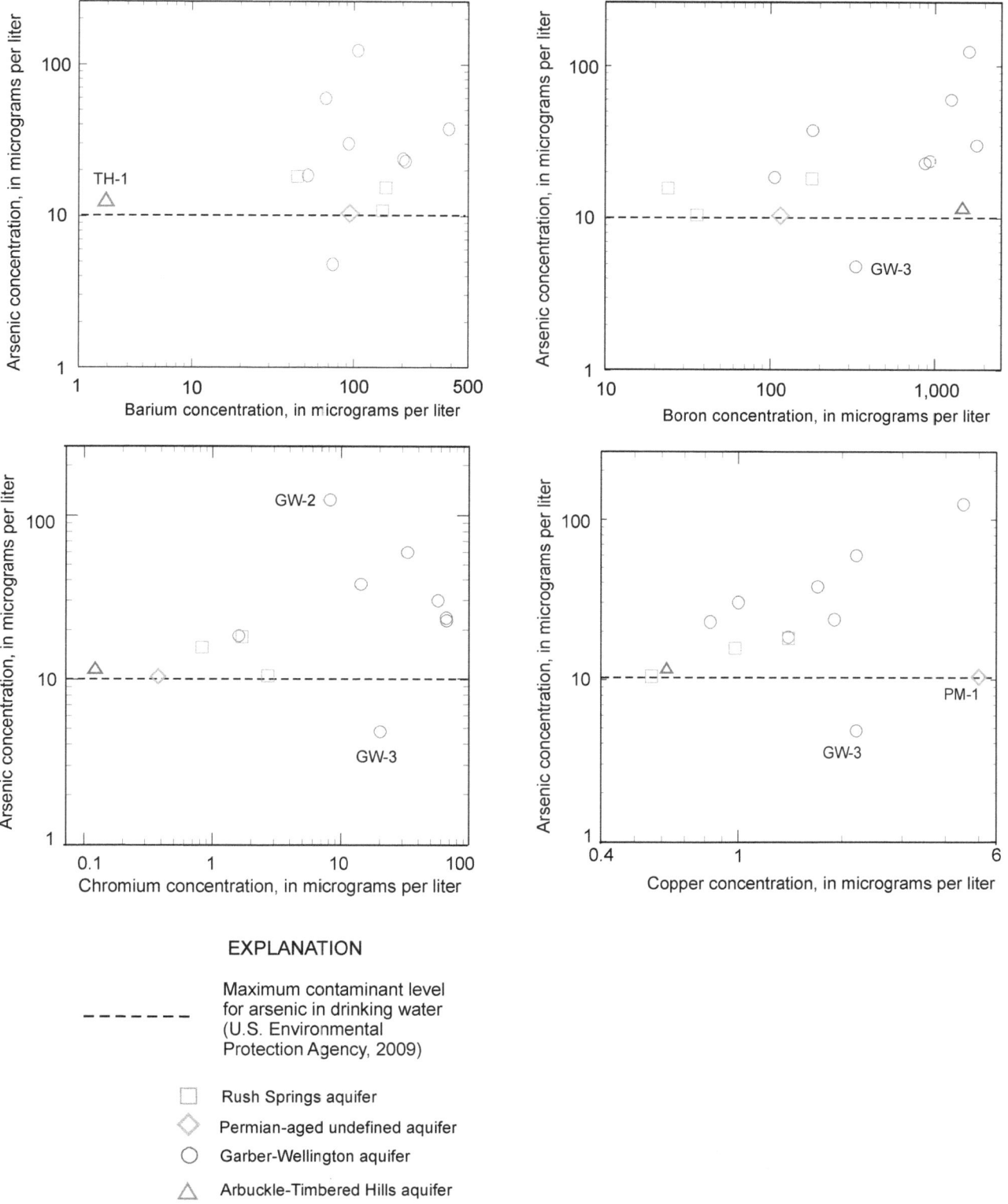

Figure 11. Relation of barium, boron, chromium, and copper with arsenic in well-head samples from production wells, Oklahoma, 2008.

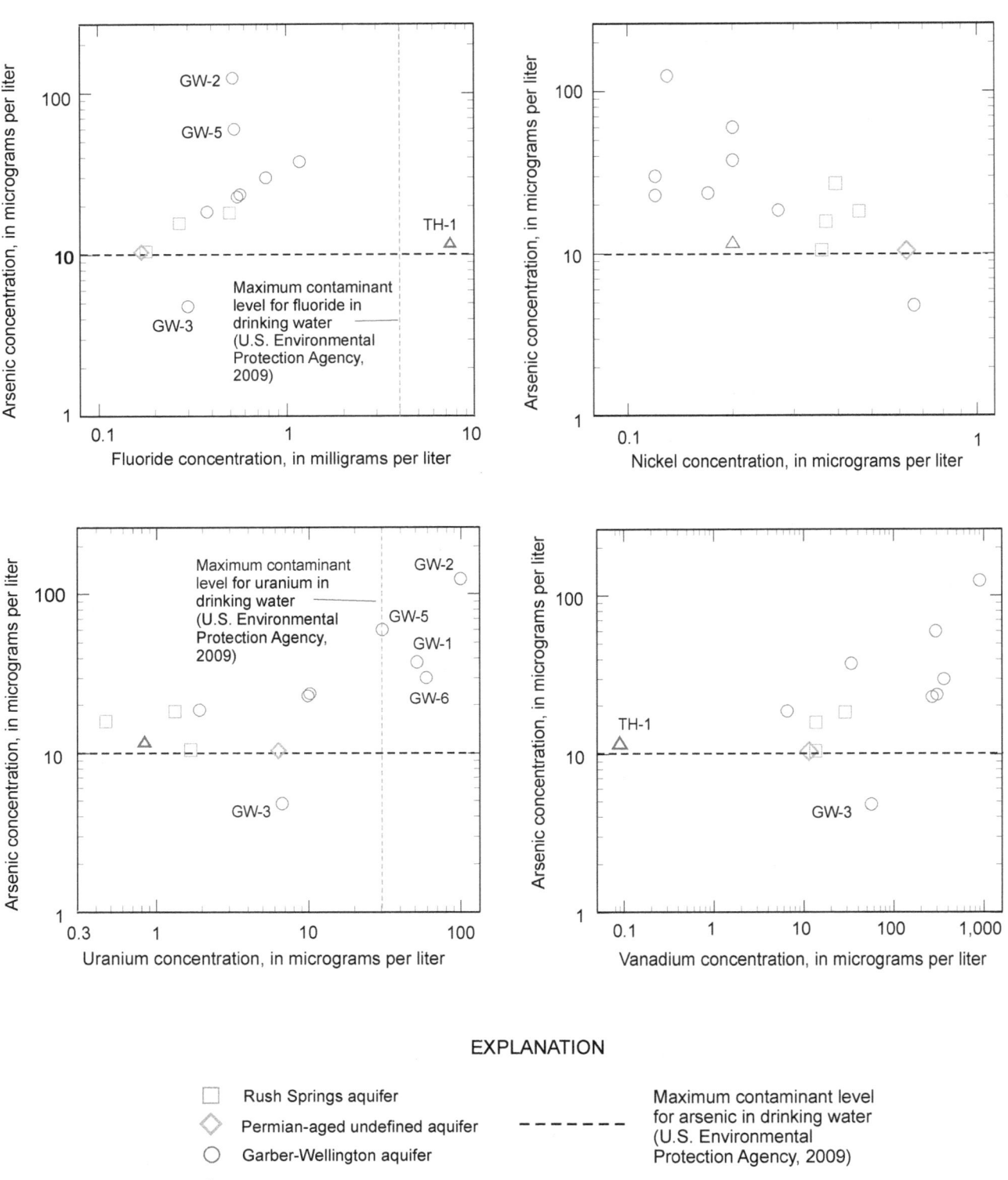

Figure 12. Relation of fluoride, nickel, uranium, and vanadium with arsenic in well-head samples from production wells, Oklahoma, 2008.

that chromium and vanadium (selenium is not shown) in addition to barium, boron, fluoride, copper, and uranium have a positive relation to arsenic in samples from most of the 12 production wells. In an oxyanion form these trace elements can compete with arsenic for sorption sites on iron oxides and be released into groundwater during similar conditions (Hem, 1992). Unlike the other trace elements, nickel showed a negative relation to arsenic (fig. 12). The sample from TH-1 tends to diverge from the trend on most plots that may be an indication of different geochemical processes occurring in the TH compared to the other aquifers. Samples from GW-2 and GW-3, which have the largest and smallest arsenic concentrations, also tend to diverge from trends on selected plots (figs. 11 and 12). Copper had a strong positive relation with arsenic except for two samples, GW-3 and PM-1 (fig. 11).

Concentrations of dissolved iron ranged from E2.0 to 10.0 µg/L in six samples and showed no correlation to arsenic in well-head samples (not shown), including water from the GW where arsenic concentrations are related to the iron oxide in the rocks. Dissolved iron has been found in previous studies to have a weak correlation with arsenic (Kresse and Fazio, 2003; Anawar and others, 2004) or similar to this study, no relation (Robertson, 1989). These findings may be the result of an association between arsenic and iron in an undissolved state. Bahadur and others (2007) showed a substantial correlation between total arsenic and total iron in a nationwide study of surface water and groundwater.

Twelve of the 21 trace elements analyzed have MCLs and six trace elements have secondary maximum contaminant levels for drinking water (table 2) (U.S. Environmental Protection Agency, 2009). Fluoride and uranium were the only trace elements, other than arsenic, that exceeded the MCLs for drinking water in well-head samples collected for the study (fig. 12). Uranium concentrations in four GW production wells (GW-1, GW-2, GW-5, and GW-6) ranged from 30.2 to 99 µg/L, exceeding the MCL of 30 µg/L for drinking water (fig. 12). Samples from GW-1, GW-2, GW-5, and GW-6 wells also had the largest arsenic concentrations measured in the study, ranging from 30 to 124 µg/L (fig. 9 and table 3).

Summary

In Oklahoma, as many as 23 public water-supply systems have been affected by the reduced arsenic maximum contaminant level of 10 µg/L for drinking water. Most large communities in Oklahoma are financially able to address noncompliant drinking water. However, many small communities and rural water districts, which operate with small resources, maintain minimal conveyance infrastructure, and often have no secondary source of water.

A project was performed by the USGS, in cooperation with the Oklahoma Department of Environmental Quality and the Groundwater Protection Council. The objective of the project was to describe arsenic-related water quality with depth in two wells by using the USGS well profiler to determine if the findings could be used to identify zones yielding water with high arsenic concentrations. If findings show that large arsenic concentrations in the borehole are related to stratigraphic zones or sedimentary layering, this technique could be considered an option in a generalized decision tree for identifying appropriate well-rehabilitation strategies that are less expensive than drilling new production wells or water treatment at the well head.

In addition, samples were collected at the well head from 12 production wells yielding water with historically large concentrations (greater than 10 µg/L) of arsenic from the Garber-Wellington aquifer, Rush Springs aquifer, and two minor aquifers; the Arbuckle-Timbered Hills aquifer in southern Oklahoma and a Permian-aged undefined aquifer in north-central Oklahoma.

The well-head and depth-dependent samples from a production well in the Rush Springs aquifer had similar water-quality characteristics but did not show any substantial changes with depth. Zones yielding noncompliant arsenic concentrations appear to be below the shallowest depth-dependent sample. However, more samples would be needed below the pump to determine whether zonal isolation would be a feasible option for this well.

Changes in water quality with depth were seen in five depth-dependent samples collected from a production well in the Garber-Wellington aquifer. The depth-dependent samples showed an increase in arsenic concentrations with depth. Data showed that most of arsenic contaminated water (about 63 percent) was entering the borehole from perforations adjacent to or below the shroud that overlies the pump. The water mixture in the borehole below the shroud was estimated to have an arsenic concentration of 36 µg/L.

Arsenic concentrations ranged from 10.4 to 124 µg/L in eleven well-head samples. Six of the seven production wells in the Garber-Wellington aquifer had the largest arsenic concentrations ranging from 18.5 to 124 µg/L. All well-head samples were oxic and arsenate was the only species of arsenic in water from 10 of the 12 production wells sampled. Arsenite was measured above the minimum reporting level in water from a production well in the Garber-Wellington aquifer and was the only arsenic species measured in water from the Arbuckle-Timbered Hills aquifer. Studies have shown that desorption from iron oxide coatings on mineral grains is the source of arsenate in the Garber-Wellington aquifer. Desorption from iron oxide also may be the source of arsenic as arsenate in groundwater samples from wells in the Rush Springs aquifer and the Permian-aged undefined aquifer. However, the source and incidence of arsenic in aquifers other than the Garber-Wellington in Oklahoma have not been studied.

Barium, boron, fluoride, chromium, copper, selenium, uranium, and vanadium showed a positive relation to arsenic in well-head samples from most of the 12 production wells. In an oxyanion form, these trace elements compete with arsenic for sorption sites on iron oxides and can be released into groundwater during similar chemical conditions as arsenic. Unlike other trace elements, nickel showed a strong inverse relation to arsenic concentrations. Iron showed no relation to arsenic in well-head samples, including water from the Garber-Wellington where arsenic concentrations are related to the iron oxide in the rocks.

Fluoride and uranium were the only trace elements, other than arsenic, that exceeded the maximum contaminant level for drinking water in well-head samples collected for the study. Uranium concentrations in four production wells in the Garber-Wellington aquifer ranged from 30.2 to 99 µg/L exceeding the maximum contaminant level of 30 µg/L for drinking water. Water from these four wells also had the largest arsenic concentrations measured in the study ranging from 30 to 124 µg/L.

References

Bahadur, Rakesh, Samuels, William, Cameron, Tara, and Smith, Ben, 2007, Assessment of the co-occurrence of drinking water contaminants: About arsenic co-occurrence, Center for Water Science and Engineering, Science Applications International Corporation. (Also available online at, *http://eh2o.saic.com/SectionProjects/EnvAnalysis/Arsenic/Arsenic.aspx.*)

Becker, M.F., and Runkle, D.L., 1998, Hydrogeology, water quality, and geochemistry of the Rush Springs aquifer, western Oklahoma: U.S. Geological Survey Water-Resources Investigations Report 98–4081, 37 p.

Beldon, Mark, 1997, Hydrologic report of the minor groundwater basins in Garfield, Grant, and Kay counties: Oklahoma Water Resources Board, Planning and Management Division, Technical Report 97–4, 21 p. (Also available online at *http://www.owrb.ok.gov/studies/reports/reports.php.*)

Bingham, R.H., and Bergman, D.L., 1980, Reconnaissance of the water resources of the Enid quadrangle north-central Oklahoma: Oklahoma Geological Survey, Hydrologic Atlas 7, 4 plates.

Cheapa Pumps, 2009, What is a submersible pump shroud or sleeve?, available online at *http://www.cheapapumps.com.au/submersible_bore_pump_shroud.html.* (Accessed March 6, 2009.)

Christenson, Scott, 1998, Ground-water-quality assessment of the Central Oklahoma aquifer—Summary of investigations, *in* Christenson, Scott, and Havens, J.S., eds., 1998, Groundwater-quality assessment of the Central Oklahoma aquifer, Oklahoma—Results of investigations: U.S. Geological Survey Water-Supply Paper 2357-A, p. 1–44.

Christenson, S.C., Morton, R.B., and Messander, B.A., 1992, Hydrogeologic maps of the Central Oklahoma aquifer,

Oklahoma: U.S. Geological Survey Hydrologic Investigations Atlas HA-724, 3 sheets, scale 1:250,000.

Driscoll, F.G., 1986, Groundwater and wells (2nd ed.): St. Paul, Minnesota, Johnson Division, 1,089 p.

Fishman, M.J., ed., 1993, Methods of analysis by the U.S. Geological Survey National Water Quality Laboratory—Determination of inorganic and organic constituents in water and fluvial sediments Method ID: I-1472-87: U.S. Geological Survey Open-File Report 93–125, 217 p.

Fishman, M.J., and Friedman, L.C., eds., 1989, Methods for determination of inorganic substances in water and fluvial sediments, Method ID: I-2327-85, I-2057-85: U.S. Geological Survey Techniques of Water-Resources Investigations, book 5, chap. A1, 545 p.

Fuller, C.C., Davis, J.A., and Waychunas, G.A., 1993, Surface chemistry of ferrihydrite—Part 2. Kinetics of arsenate adsorption and coprecipitation: Geochimica et Cosmochimica Acta, v. 51, p. 2,271–2,282. (Also available online at *http://www.sciencedirect.com/science?_ob=MiamiImageURL&_imagekey=B6V66-489SJYK-BN-1&_cdi=5806&_user=696292&_check=y&_orig=search&_coverDate=05%2F31%2F1993&view=c&wchp=dGLbVzz-zSkWz&md5=da661cd1fc1e0cf3d5034f737f3e0440&ie=/sdarticle.pdf.*)

Garbarino, J.R., 1999, Methods of analysis by the U.S. Geological Survey National Water Quality Laboratory—Determination of dissolved arsenic, boron, lithium, selenium, strontium, thallium, and vanadium using inductively coupled plasma-mass spectrometry, Method ID: I-2477-92: U.S. Geological Survey Open-File Report 99–093, 31 p.

Garbarino, J.R., Bednar, A.J., and Burkhardt, M.R., 2002, Methods of analysis by the U.S. Geological Survey National Water Quality Laboratory—Arsenic speciation in natural-water samples using laboratory and field methods, Method ID: I-2191-02: U.S. Geological Survey Water-Resources Investigations Report 02–4144, 40 p.

Garbarino, J.R., Kanagy, L.K., and Cree, M.E., 2006, Determination of elements in natural water, biota, sediment and soil samples using collision/reaction cell inductively coupled plasma-mass spectrometry, Method ID: I-2020-05: U.S. Geological Survey Techniques and Methods, book 5, chap. B1, 88 p.

Gromadzki, Gregory A., 2004, Outcrop-based gamma-ray characterization of arsenic-bearing lithofacies in the Garber-Wellington formation, Central Oklahoma aquifer, Cleveland County, Oklahoma: Stillwater, Oklahoma State University, Master's thesis, 231 p.

Harrington, John, and Roberts, Jim, 2005, Arsenic mapping in Garber-Wellington aquifer: Association of Central Oklahoma Governments, Water Resources Division, Grant Number: 604(b), FY: 2002, 85 p.

Havens, J.S., 1977, Reconnaissance of the water resources of the Lawton quadrangle, southwestern Oklahoma: Oklahoma Geological Survey Hydrologic Atlas 6, 4 sheets, scale 1:250,000.

Havens, John S., 1983, Reconnaissance of ground water in vicinity of Wichita Mountains southwestern Oklahoma: Oklahoma Geological Survey, Circular 85, 13 p.

Hem, J.D., 1992, Study and interpretation of the chemical characteristics of natural water (3d ed.): U.S. Geological Survey Water-Supply Paper 2254, 263 p.

Hinkle, S.R., and Polette, D.J., 1998, Arsenic in ground water of the Willamette Basin, Oregon: U.S. Geological Survey Water-Resources Investigations Report 98–4205, 34 p.

Izbicki, J.A., Christenson, A.H., Hanson, R.T., Martin, Peter, Crawford, S.M., and Smith, G.A., 1999, U.S. Geological Survey combined well-bore flow and depth-dependent water sampler: U.S. Geological Survey Fact Sheet 196–99, 2 p.

Izbicki, J.A., Stamos, C.L., Metzger, L.F., Halford, K.J., Kulp, T.R., and Bennet, G.L., 2008, Source, distribution, and management of arsenic in water from wells, eastern San Joaquin ground-water subbasin, California: U.S. Geological Survey Open File Report 2008–1272, 8 p.

Keys, Scott W., 2005, Borehole geophysics applied to ground-water investigations; Nuclear logging, U.S. Geological Survey, Techniques of Water-Resources Investigations, book 2, chap. E-2, sec. 5, p. 79–82, available online at *http://pubs.usgs.gov/twri/twri2-e2/html/pdf.html*.

Keys, Scott W., 2005a, Borehole geophysics applied to ground-water investigations; Electric logging, U.S. Geological Survey, Techniques of Water-Resources Investigations, book 2, chap. E-2, sec. 4, p. 6, available online at *http://pubs.usgs.gov/twri/twri2-e2/html/pdf.html*.

Keys, Scott W., 2005b, Borehole geophysics applied to ground-water investigations; Caliper logging U.S. Geological Survey, Techniques of Water-Resources Investigations, book 2, chap. E-2, sec. 6, p. 119–122, available online at *http://pubs.usgs.gov/twri/twri2-e2/html/pdf.html*.

Kreese, Tim, and Fazio, John, 2003, Occurrence of arsenic in groundwaters of Arkansas and implications for source and release mechanisms: Arkansas ambient ground-water monitoring program, Arkansas Department of Environmental Quality, Water Quality Report WQ 03-03-01, 35 p.

Parkhurst, D.L., Christenson, S.C., and Breit, G.N., 1996, Ground-water-quality assessment of the Central Oklahoma aquifer, Oklahoma–Geochemical and geohydrologic investigations: U.S. Geological Survey Water-Supply Paper 2357-C, 101 p.

Piper, A.M., 1944, A graphic procedure in the geochemical interpretation of water analyses: Transactions, American Geophysical Union, v. 25, p. 914–923.

Robertson, F.N., 1989, Arsenic in ground-water under oxidizing conditions, south-west United States: Journal of Environmental Geochemistry and Health, p. 171–185. (Also available online at *http://www.springerlink.com/content/t36747742478t515/*.)

Rounds, S.A., and Wilde, F.D., eds., 2001, Alkalinity and acid neutralizing capacity (2nd ed.): U.S. Geological Survey Techniques of Water-Resources Investigations, book 9, chap. A6, section 6.6, available online at *http://pubs.water.usgs.gov/twri9A6/*. (Accessed April 3, 2003.)

Sandstrom, Mark W., and Lewis, James A., 2009, Instructions for field use of spike solutions for organic-analyte samples; *in* Wilde, F.D., Radtke, D.B., Gibs, Jacob, and Iwatsubo, R.T., eds., 2004 with updates through 2009, Processing of water samples (version 2.2): U.S. Geological Survey Techniques of Water-Resources Investigations, book 9, chap. A5.

Schlottmann, J.L., Mosier, E.L., and Breit, G.N., 1998, Arsenic, chromium, selenium, and uranium in the Central Oklahoma aquifer, *in* Christenson, Scott, and Havens, J.S., eds., Ground-water quality assessment of the Central Oklahoma aquifer, Oklahoma—Results of investigations: U.S. Geological Survey Water-Supply Paper 2357-A, p. 119–179.

Smith, A.H., Hopenhayn-Rich, Claudia, Bates, M.N., Goeden, H.M., Hertz-Picciotto, Irva, Duggan, H.M., Wood, R., Kosnett, M.J., and Smith, M.T., 1992, Cancer risks from arsenic in drinking water: Environmental Health Perspectives, v. 97, p. 259–267.

Smith, S.J., Paxton, S.T., Christenson, Scott, Puls, R.W., and Greer, J.R., 2009, Flow contribution and water quality with depth in a test hole and public-supply wells—Implications for arsenic remediation through well modification, Norman, Oklahoma, 2003–2006: U.S. Environmental Protection Agency, EPA 600/R-09/036, 57 p. (Also available online at *http://www.epa.gov/nrmrl/pubs/600r09036/600r09036.pdf*.)

Sracek, Ondra, Prosun, Bhattachara, Jacks, Gunnar, Gustafsson, Jon-Petter, and von Bromssen, Mattias, 2004, Behavior of arsenic and geochemical modeling of arsenic enrichment in aqueous environments: Applied Geochemistry, v. 19, 2004, p. 169–180.

Stollenwerk, K.G., 2003, Geochemical processes controlling transport of arsenic in groundwater—A review of adsorption, *in* Welch, A.H., and Stollenwerk, K.G., eds., Arsenic in ground water: Geochemistry and occurrence: Boston, Kluwer Academic Publishers, 34 p.

Tanaka, H.H., and Davis, L.V., 1963, Ground-water resources of the Rush Springs Sandstone in the Caddo County area, Oklahoma: Oklahoma Geological Survey Circular 61, 63 p.

Timme, P.J., 1995, National Water Quality Laboratory 1995 services catalog: U.S. Geological Survey Open-File Report 95–352, p. 92.

U.S. Environmental Protection Agency, 2001, National primary drinking-water regulations: Arsenic and clarifications to compliance and new source contaminants monitoring—Final rule: Federal Register, vol. 66, no. 14, p. 6,975–7,066. (Also available online at, *http://www.epa.gov/fedrgstr/EPA-WATER/2001/January/Day-22/w1668.htm.*)

U.S. Environmental Protection Agency, 2002, Proven alternatives for aboveground treatment of arsenic in groundwater: U.S. Environmental Protection Agency, Office of Solid Waste and Emergency Response, EPA-542-S-02-002, 63 p.

U.S. Environmental Protection Agency, 2009, Drinking water contaminants, National primary drinking water regulations and national secondary drinking water regulations. (Also available online at *http://www.epa.gov/safewater/contaminants/index.html#sec.*)

U.S. Geological Survey, 2006, Collection of water samples (ver. 2.0): U.S. Geological Survey Techniques of Water-Resources Investigations, book 9, chap. A4, available online at *http://pubs.water.usgs.gov/twri9A4/.*

Welch, A.H., Westjohn, D.B., Helsel, D.R., and Wanty, R.B., 2000, Arsenic in ground water of the United States: Occurrence and geochemistry: Ground Water, v. 38, no. 4, p. 589–604.

Wilde, F.D., and Radtke, D.B., eds., 1998, Methods for field measurements: U.S. Geological Survey Techniques of Water Resources Investigations, book 9, chap. A6.0-A6.6, 135 p.

Wilde, F.D., Radtke, D.B., Gibs, Jacob, and Iwatsubo, R.T., eds., 2004 with updates through 2009, Processing of water samples (ver. 2.2): U.S. Geological Survey Techniques of Water-Resources Investigations, book 9, chap. A5, available online at *http://pubs.water.usgs.gov/twri9A5/.*

Wilde, F.D., ed., 2004, Cleaning of Equipment for water sampling (ver. 2.0): U.S. Geological Survey Techniques of Water-Resources Investigations, book 9, chap. A3, available on line at *http://pubs.water.usgs.gov/twri9A3/.*

World Health Organization, 2001, Arsenic in drinking water: Fact Sheet 210, Revised May 2001, available online at *http://www.who.int/mediacentre/factsheets/fs210/en/print. html.* (Accessed January 11, 2008.)

Appendix 1—Water-Property Measurements and Chemical-Constituent Concentrations Measured in Water from Depth-Dependent and Well-Head Samples, Oklahoma, 2008

Appendix 1. Water-property measurements and chemical-constituent concentrations measured in water from depth-dependent and well-head samples, Oklahoma, 2008. All concentrations are dissolved unless otherwise noted.

[USGS, U.S. Geological Survey; ID, identifier; E, estimated; <, less than; --, not available; mg/L, milligram per liter; µg/L, microgram per liter; µS/cm, microsiemens per centimeter; °C, degrees Celsius; GW, Garber-Wellington aquifer; PM, Permian-aged undefined aquifer; RS, Rush Springs aquifer; TH, Arbuckle Timbered Hills aquifer; lds, land surface; WH, well-head sample; DMA, dimethylarsinate; MMA, monomethylarsonate; c, sample was contaminated and constituent was not measured]

USGS site ID	Well ID	Date	Time	Aquifer	Sample type	Well depth (feet below lds)	Sample location (feet below land surface)	Dissolved oxygen (mg/L)	pH
355110097240301	GW-1	Oct. 28, 2008	1100	GW	Regular	--	WH	2.3	8.8
355034097145201	GW-2	Oct. 9, 2008	1030	GW	Regular	310	WH	3.2	7.8
353308097290701	GW-3	Aug. 7, 2008	1200	GW	Regular	750	WH	6.0	8.0
353308097290701	GW-3	Aug. 7, 2008	1201	GW	Replicate	750	WH	--	--
353308097290701	GW-3	Sep. 11, 2008	1030	GW	Regular	750	WH	5.0	7.6
352934097271502	GW-4	Jul. 25, 2008	1130	GW	Regular	265	WH	3.8	7.1
352604097370901	GW-5	Jul. 22, 2008	1100	GW	Regular	854	WH	2.9	8.5
352604097370901	GW-5	Aug. 29, 2008	1345	GW	Regular	854	WH	--	8.6
351914097320201	GW-6	Jul. 16, 2008	1500	GW	Regular	782	WH	4.0	8.6
351853097284701	GW-7X	Dec. 12, 2008	1000	GW	Regular	811	WH	8.6	8.7
351853097284701	GW-7X	Dec. 13, 2008	1100	GW	Regular	811	582	7.7	7.8
351853097284701	GW-7X	Dec. 13, 2008	0800	GW	Regular	811	610	5.3	8.0
351853097284701	GW-7X	Dec. 12, 2008	1430	GW	Regular	811	653	7.2	8.2
351853097284701	GW-7X	Dec. 12, 2008	1330	GW	Regular	811	686	8.4	8.1
351853097284701	GW-7X	Dec. 12, 2008	1030	GW	Regular	811	710	8.5	8.1
351853097284701	GW-7X	Dec. 13, 2008	1500	GW	Replicate	811	WH	8.3	8.7
364824097311601	PM-1	Jul. 31, 2008	1300	PM	Regular	120	WH	6.1	6.9
353237098403901	RS-1	Jul. 15, 2008	1100	RS	Regular	320	WH	8.6	7.4
352822098233801	RS-2X	Nov. 25, 2008	1600	RS	Regular	294	285	7.0	7.2
352822098233801	RS-2X	Nov. 25, 2008	1630	RS	Regular	294	WH	9.2	7.2
352822098233801	RS-2X	Nov. 25, 2008	1700	RS	Regular	294	275	10.2	7.3
352822098233801	RS-2X	Nov. 26, 2008	1300	RS	Regular	294	267	15.4	7.4
352822098233801	RS-2X	Nov. 26, 2008	1301	RS	Replicate	294	267	--	--
351754098331501	RS-3	Sep. 5, 2008	1030	RS	Regular	375	WH	10.7	7.4
343706098451201	TH-1	Sep. 5, 2008	1400	TH	Regular	620	WH	3.7	9.0

Appendix 1. Water-property measurements and chemical-constituent concentrations measured in water from depth-dependent and well-head samples, Oklahoma, 2008. All concentrations are dissolved unless otherwise noted.—Continued

[USGS, U.S. Geological Survey; ID, identifier; E, estimated; <, less than; --, not available; mg/L, milligram per liter; µg/L, microgram per liter; µS/cm, microsiemens per centimeter; °C, degrees Celsius; GW, Garber-Wellington aquifer; PM, Permian-aged undefined aquifer; RS, Rush Springs aquifer; TH, Arbuckle Timbered Hills aquifer; lds, land surface; WH, well-head sample; DMA, dimethylarsinate; MMA, monomethylarsonate; c, sample was contaminated and constituent was not measured]

USGS site ID	Well ID	Specific conductance (µS/cm)	Temperature (°C)	Calcium (mg/L)	Magnesium (mg/L)	Potassium (mg/L)	Sodium (mg/L)	Alkalinity (mg/L)	Bicarbonate (mg/L)	Carbonate (mg/L)	Bromide (µg/L)	Chloride (mg/L)	Fluoride (mg/L)	Silica (mg/L)	Sulfate (mg/L)	Total dissolved solids (mg/L)	Aluminum (µg/L)	Antimony (µg/L)	Arsenate (µg/L)
355110097240301	GW-1	742	17.9	2.02	0.877	0.48	173	300	342	11	0.08	42.4	0.78	8.90	29.4	440	8.3	E.03	28.1
355034097145201	GW-2	1,010	18	20.3	12.9	.87	211	494	599	2	.14	21.8	.52	11.4	24	602	<4	E.02	125
353308097290701	GW-3	665	18.3	25	20.3	1.99	82.3	209	251	2	.05	59.2	.30	14	35	365	E1.6	<.14	c
353308097290701	GW-3	--	--	24	19.6	1.97	87.4	--	--	--	.05	58.3	.28	13.7	34.5	--	E.8	<.14	c
353308097290701	GW-3	732	18	--	--	--	--	206	250	0	--	--	--	--	--	--	--	--	<.8
352934097271502	GW-4	919	18.1	72.5	28.3	2.02	88.3	355	433	0	.12	52.1	.38	16.7	70	545	2	<.14	16.2
352604097370901	GW-5	681	19.7	--	--	--	--	283	337	4	--	--	--	--	--	--	--	--	53.5
352604097370901	GW-5	--	--	7.34	2.42	.57	159	283	329	8	.04	16.1	.53	10.5	63.9	--	1.9	<.14	59.9
351914097320201	GW-6	982	19.7	10.6	8.85	1.31	191	312	362	9	.19	125	1.18	11.8	17.6	555	2.3	<.14	36.7
351853097284701	GW-7X	504	18.5	10.5	8.55	1.21	100	258	305	4	.03	6.22	.55	11.7	11.3	307	E2.2	<.04	20.9
351853097284701	GW-7X	377	13.0	20.9	19.8	1.91	43	210	254	9	.04	7.53	.33	13.4	7.20	249	<4	<.04	<.8
351853097284701	GW-7X	404	12.4	13.9	12.3	1.56	63.5	200	E241	E1	.02	7.37	.31	12.8	7.11	239	<4	<.04	E.5
351853097284701	GW-7X	408	12.4	14.9	13.2	1.58	58.8	203	246	0	.02	7.21	.33	12.9	7.19	239	<4	<.04	E.7
351853097284701	GW-7X	405	13.4	14.9	13.3	1.61	60.1	205	249	0	E.02	7.39	.32	13	7.46	242	E4	<.04	E.7
351853097284701	GW-7X	404	10.8	14.6	13.2	1.59	61.4	209	252	1	.02	7.20	.32	12.9	7.24	245	E3.3	<.04	1.2
351853097284701	GW-7X	509	18.7	10.2	8.27	1.15	102	326	378	10	.02	6.12	.57	11.9	11.5	349	E2.4	<.04	21.9
364824097311601	PM-1	1,630	16.9	145	40.7	1.18	140	418	510	0	.68	216	.17	32.9	108	937	<1.6	<.14	9.7
353237099840301	RS-1	758	17.8	105	13.2	1.30	31.4	127	154	0	.20	14.3	.50	21.2	219	483	<1.6	<.14	17.2
352822098233801	RS-2X	634	16.8	64.5	8.04	1.31	60	290	353	0	.03	16.5	.18	32.4	26.2	384	<4	.06	9.2
352822098233801	RS-2X	659	17.1	73.4	9.23	1.42	63.3	281	342	0	.03	17.8	.18	26.8	41.2	402	<4	E.03	9.3
352822098233801	RS-2X	626	11.1	71.6	9.01	1.36	62.6	286	348	0	.04	17.6	.17	30.5	25.5	390	<4	E.03	9.5
352822098233801	RS-2X	672	10.2	67.7	7.34	1.56	82	--	--	--	.02	16.9	.16	29.2	21.7	--	10.3	.05	6.3
352822098233801	RS-2X	--	--	66.2	7.23	1.56	82.7	--	--	--	.02	17	.17	24.2	21.8	--	<4	.06	6.2
351754098331501	RS-3	328	18.1	41.6	9.76	.90	10.1	157	191	0	.06	5.03	.27	20.9	6.61	191	E1.3	<.14	14.4
343706098451201	TH-1	875	19.7	1.38	.473	.78	200	303	343	13	.19	51	7.44	9.31	57.4	511	3.5	<.14	<.8

Appendix 1.   Water-property measurements and chemical-constituent concentrations measured in water from depth-dependent and well-head samples, Oklahoma, 2008. All concentrations are dissolved unless otherwise noted.—Continued

[USGS, U.S. Geological Survey; ID, identifier; E, estimated; <, less than; --, not available; mg/L, milligram per liter; µg/L, microgram per liter; µS/cm, microsiemens per centimeter; °C, degrees Celsius; GW, Garber-Wellington aquifer; PM, Permian-aged undefined aquifer; RS, Rush Springs aquifer; TH, Arbuckle Timbered Hills aquifer; lds, land surface; WH, well-head sample; DMA, dimethylarsinate; MMA, monomethylarsonate; c, sample was contaminated and constituent was not measured]

USGS site ID	Well ID	Arsenic dissolved (µg/L)	Arsenic total (µg/L)	Arsenite (µg/L)	Barium (µg/L)	Beryllium (µg/L)	Boron (µg/L)	Cadmium (µg/L)	Chromium (µg/L)	Cobalt (µg/L)	Copper (µg/L)	Iron (µg/L)	Lead (µg/L)	Lithium (µg/L)	Manganese (µg/L)	Molybdenum (µg/L)	Nickel (µg/L)	Selenium (µg/L)
355110097240301	GW-1	30	27.8	<0.8	93	<0.02	1,780	0.02	56.8	<0.02	<1.0	<4	0.11	7.2	<0.2	4	<0.12	49.6
355034097145201	GW-2	124	111	<.8	106	E.01	1,600	E.01	8.2	E.02	4.5	E2	.51	9.4	<.2	1.7	.13	3.1
353308097290701	GW-3	4.8	4.7	c	74	<.01	330	<.04	20.2	E.02	2.2	<8	.18	7.2	.4	.9	.66	2
353308097290701	GW-3	4.7	4.6	c	75	<.01	303	<.04	20.4	E.02	1.8	E8	.17	6.4	.4	.8	E.15	2
353308097290701	GW-3	1	1	<.6	--	--	--	--	--	--	--	--	--	--	--	--	--	--
352934097271502	GW-4	18.5	18.0	1.5	52	<.01	106	<.04	1.6	.05	1.4	<8	1.14	18.4	27.6	1	.27	.52
352604097370901	GW-5	--	--	<.6	--	--	--	--	--	--	--	--	--	--	--	--	--	--
352604097370901	GW-5	59.9	57.9	<1.2	67	E.01	1,250	<.04	32.8	<.02	2.2	<8	E.07	9.5	.6	6.1	<.20	31.1
351914097320201	GW-6	37.7	35.3	<.6	385	.01	181	.05	14.3	<.02	1.7	<8	.17	9.3	E.2	25	<.20	49.4
351853097284701	GW-7X	22.9	21.9	<.8	208	<.02	868	<.02	66.2	E.01	E.83	5	.23	6.6	E.2	3.4	<.12	25.8
351853097284701	GW-7X	.49	.60	<.8	316	<.02	236	<.02	44.2	.03	<1.0	E4	E.04	7.3	.7	.4	.50	.8
351853097284701	GW-7X	.65	.64	<.8	282	<.02	266	<.02	45.9	.02	<1.0	E3	.09	7.9	.4	.4	.32	.93
351853097284701	GW-7X	.85	.86	<.8	291	<.02	255	<.02	44.4	E.02	<1.0	<4.0	<.06	7.8	.2	.3	.27	.94
351853097284701	GW-7X	.90	.86	<.8	290	<.02	255	<.02	44.8	.02	<1.0	E3	E.04	7.8	.2	.3	.28	.96
351853097284701	GW-7X	1.4	1.4	<.8	284	<.02	277	<.02	45.5	.02	<1.0	5	.09	8.0	.4	.4	.31	1.6
351853097284701	GW-7X	23.7	22.9	<.8	202	<.02	927	E.01	66	E.01	1.9	5	.24	6.6	E.2	3.5	.17	25
364824097311601	PM-1	10.4	10.1	<.6	97	<.01	115	<.04	.38	.07	5.0	<8	.94	34.2	<.2	.7	.63	8.9
353237098403901	RS-1	18.2	17.5	<.6	47	<.01	179	<.04	1.7	.05	1.4	10	.37	14.4	1.0	3	.46	.4
352822098233801	RS-2X	10.1	9.7	<.8	162	<.02	35	<.02	2.9	.05	<1.0	<4	.25	17.3	.9	.1	.70	.69
352822098233801	RS-2X	10.5	9.9	<.8	148	<.02	36	<.02	2.7	.04	E.56	E3	.32	17.1	<.2	.1	.36	.83
352822098233801	RS-2X	10.4	10	<.8	155	<.02	34	<.02	2.5	.04	<1.0	<4	.14	16.3	.5	.1	.51	.82
352822098233801	RS-2X	7.1	7.7	<.8	147	<.02	31	<.02	3.8	.05	<1.0	E4	.19	17.6	.8	.1	.69	.55
352822098233801	RS-2X	7.1	7.7	<.8	144	<.02	33	E.01	3.9	.06	3.8	7	1.33	18.9	.9	.1	.80	.59
351754098331501	RS-3	15.7	15	<.6	154	<.01	24	<.04	.83	.04	E.98	<8	.51	6.2	<.2	.5	.37	.24
343706098451201	TH-1	11.6	10.8	10.8	3	.01	1,470	E.03	<.12	<.02	E.62	E7	.13	22.2	.5	14.4	<.20	<.04

Appendix 1.   Water-property measurements and chemical-constituent concentrations measured in water from depth-dependent and well-head samples, Oklahoma, 2008. All concentrations are dissolved unless otherwise noted.—Continued

[USGS, U.S. Geological Survey; ID, identifier; E, estimated; <, less than; --, not available; mg/L, milligram per liter; µg/L, microgram per liter; µS/cm, microsiemens per centimeter; °C, degrees Celsius; GW, Garber-Wellington aquifer; PM, Permian-aged undefined aquifer; RS, Rush Springs aquifer; TH, Arbuckle Timbered Hills aquifer; lds, land surface; WH, well-head sample; DMA, dimethylarsinate; MMA, monomethylarsonate; c, sample was contaminated and constituent was not measured]

USGS site ID	Well ID	Silver (µg/L)	Strontium (µg/L)	Thorium (µg/L)	Vanadium (µg/L)	Zinc (µg/L)	DMA (µg/L)	MMA (µg/L)	Uranium (µg/L)
355110097240301	GW-1	<0.008	55.6	<0.04	361	E1.7	<0.6	<1.8	58.8
355034097145201	GW-2	<.008	237	<.04	901	4.6	<.6	<1.8	99
353308097290701	GW-3	<.1	1,000	<.04	55.9	3.3	c	c	6.63
353308097290701	GW-3	<.1	1,020	<.04	54.2	3.1	c	c	6.62
353308097290701	GW-3	--	--	--	--	--	<.6	<1.8	--
352934097271502	GW-4	<.1	678	<.04	6.5	4.2	<.6	<1.8	1.9
352604097370901	GW-5	--	--	--	--	--	<.6	<1.8	--
352604097370901	GW-5	<.1	140	<.04	293	E1.6	<1.2	<3.6	30.2
351914097320201	GW-6	<.1	373	<.04	33.7	3.6	<.6	<1.8	51
351853097284701	GW-7X	<.008	331	<.04	267	<2	<.6	<1.8	9.79
351853097284701	GW-7X	<.008	661	<.04	8.3	<2	<.6	<1.8	4.61
351853097284701	GW-7X	<.008	440	<.04	7.9	<2	<.6	<1.8	4.08
351853097284701	GW-7X	<.008	466	<.04	10.8	<2	<.6	<1.8	4.16
351853097284701	GW-7X	<.008	467	<.04	11.8	<2	<.6	<1.8	4.14
351853097284701	GW-7X	<.008	467	<.04	16.5	<2	<.6	<1.8	4.38
351853097284701	GW-7X	<.008	317	<.04	302	E1.8	<.6	<1.8	10.1
364824097311601	PM-1	<.1	937	<.04	11.4	12.7	<.6	<1.8	6.28
353237098403901	RS-1	<.1	925	<.04	28.8	3.3	<.6	<1.8	1.31
352822098233801	RS-2X	<.008	208	<.04	13.4	3.9	<.6	<1.8	1.16
352822098233801	RS-2X	<.008	266	<.04	13.5	2	<.6	<1.8	1.66
352822098233801	RS-2X	<.008	203	<.04	12.5	9	<.6	<1.8	1.22
352822098233801	RS-2X	<.008	119	<.04	14.3	3.2	<.6	<1.8	.54
352822098233801	RS-2X	<.008	121	<.04	14.5	10.4	<.6	<1.8	.54
351754098331501	RS-3	<.1	1,220	<.04	13.6	30.9	<.6	<1.8	.46
343706098451201	TH-1	<.1	26.1	<.04	.09	1.8	<.6	<1.8	.83

Appendix 2—Concentrations of Equipment-Blank Sample and Analytical Relative Percent Difference for Chemical Constituents Measured in Replicate Samples from Depth-Dependent and Well-Head Samples, Oklahoma, 2008

Appendix 2. Concentrations of equipment-blank sample and analytical relative percent difference of chemical constituents replicate samples for measured in water from depth-dependent and well-head samples, Oklahoma, 2008. Unless noted, all concentrations are dissolved.

[USGS, U.S. Geological Survey; <, constituent was not detected or concentration was less than the reporting level; E, estimated; mg/L, milligram per liter; μg/L, microgram per liter; na, not analyzed; DMA, dimethylarsinate; MMA, monomethylarsonate; --, not calculated; Relative percent difference values were not calculated if one constituent had an estimated concentration or a concentration less than the reporting level; c, sample was contaminated and constituent was not measured]

USGS station identifier	Well identifier	Date	Sample type	Calcium, (mg/L)	Magnesium, (mg/L)	Potassium, (mg/L)	Sodium, (mg/L)	Bromide (μg/L)
352822098233801	RS-2X	Nov. 26, 2008	Sample	67.7	7.34	1.56	82.0	0.02
352822098233801	RS-2X	Nov. 26, 2008	Replicate	66.2	7.23	1.56	82.7	.02
Relative percent difference				2.2	1.5	0	-.8	0
353308097290701	GW-3	Aug. 7, 2008	Sample	25.0	20.3	1.99	82.3	.05
353308097290701	GW-3	Aug. 7, 2008	Replicate	24.0	19.6	1.97	87.4	.05
Relative percent difference				4.1	3.5	1.0	-6.0	0
Equipment blank				.04	<.02	<.02	<.12	<.02
Spiked sample from GW-3	GW-3	Aug. 7, 2008		na	na	na	na	na

USGS station identifier	Well identifier	Chloride (mg/L)	Fluoride (mg/L)	Silica (mg/L)	Sulfate (mg/L)	Aluminum (μg/L)	Antimony (μg/L)	Arsenate arsenic (μg/L)	Arsenic, dissolved (μg/L)	Arsenic total (μg/L)	Arsenite arsenic (μg/L)	Barium (μg/L)
352822098233801	RS-2X	16.9	0.16	29.2	21.7	10.3	0.05	6.3	7.1	7.7	<0.8	147
352822098233801	RS-2X	17.0	.17	24.2	21.8	<4.0	.06	6.2	7.1	7.7	<.8	144
Relative percent difference		-.6	-6.1	19	-.5	--	-18	1.6	0	0	--	2.1
353308097290701	GW-3	59.2	.30	14.0	35.0	E1.6	<.14	c	4.8	4.7	c	74
353308097290701	GW-3	58.3	.28	13.7	34.5	E.8	<.14	c	4.7	4.6	c	75
Relative percent difference		1.5	6.9	2.2	1.4	--	--	-10	2.1	2.2	-12.4	-1.3
Equipment blank		<.12	E.07	E.02	<.18	E1.2	<.1	--	<.06	<.6	--	E.2
Spiked sample from GW-3	GW-3	na	na	na	na	na	na	31.5	na	na	17.5	na

Appendix 2.   Concentrations of equipment-blank sample and analytical relative percent difference of chemical constituents replicate samples for measured in water from depth-dependent and well-head samples, Oklahoma, 2008. Unless noted, all concentrations are dissolved.—Continued

[USGS, U.S. Geological Survey; <, constituent was not detected or concentration was less than the reporting level; E, estimated; mg/L, milligram per liter; µg/L, microgram per liter; na, not analyzed; DMA, dimethylarsinate; MMA, monomethylarsonate; --, not calculated; Relative percent difference values were not calculated if one constituent had an estimated concentration or a concentration less than the reporting level; c, sample was contaminated and constituent was not measured]

USGS station identifier	Well identifier	Beryllium (µg/L)	Boron (µg/L)	Cadmium (µg/L)	Chromium (µg/L)	Cobalt (µg/L)	Copper (µg/L)	Iron (µg/L)	Lead (µg/L)	Lithium (µg/L)	Manganese (µg/L)	Molybdenum (µg/L)	Nickel (µg/L)
352822098233801	RS-2X	<0.02	31	<0.02	3.8	0.05	<1.0	E4	0.19	17.6	0.80	0.1	0.69
352822098233801	RS-2X	<.02	33	E.01	3.9	.06	3.8	7	1.33	18.9	.9	.1	.80
Relative percent difference		--	-6.25	--	-2.6	-18.2	--	--	-150	-7.1	-11.8	0	-14.8
353308097290701	GW-3	<.01	330	<.04	20.2	E.02	2.2	<8	.18	7.2	.4	.9	.66
353308097290701	GW-3	<.01	303	<.04	20.4	E.02	1.8	E8	.17	6.4	.4	.8	E.15
Relative percent difference		--	8.5	--	-1.0	--	20	--	5.7	11.8	0	11.8	--
Equipment blank		<.008	<6	<.04	<.1	<.02	1.06	<8	.39	<1	<.2	<.2	E.18
Spike sample from GW-3	GW-3	na	na	na	na	na	na	na	na	na	na	na	na

USGS station identifier	Well identifier	Selenium, (µg/L)	Silica, (µg/L)	Strontium, (µg/L)	Thallium, (µg/L)	Vanadium, (µg/L)	Zinc, (µg/L)	DMA, (µg/L)	MMA, (µg/L)	Uranium, (µg/L)
352822098233801	RS-2X	0.55	<0.008	119	<0.04	14.3	3.2	<0.6	<1.8	0.54
352822098233801	RS-2X	.59	<.008	121	<.04	14.5	10.4	<.6	<1.8	.54
Relative percent difference		-7.0	--	-1.7	--	-1.4	-105.9	--	--	0
353308097290701	GW-3	2.0	<.1	1,000	<.04	55.9	3.3	c	c	6.63
353308097290701	GW-3	2.0	<.1	1,020	<.04	54.2	3.1	c	c	6.62
Relative percent difference		0	--	-2.0	--	3.1	6.2	--	--	.1
Equipment blank		<.04	E.02	<.8	<.04	<.04	5.3	na	na	<.02
Spiked sample from GW-3	GW-3	na	na	na	na	na	na	22.1	21.9	na

Publishing support provided by
Lafayette Publishing Service Center